DAILY DEVOTIONAL
FOR
GIRLS

3-MINUTE DEVOTIONS FOR GIRLS 10-12

by

Denise Gilmore

ADISAN Publishing AB

INTRODUCTION

This yearlong devotional is designed to help you learn how to get, develop, maintain, and keep a relationship with Jesus as your Lord and Savior. Excitement, trials, tribulation, doubt, fear, and other emotions lie ahead,
but you can rest assured that God has you in His hands.

Even though people in your life will fail you at certain times, Jesus will never fail you. You will learn what it means to stay close to Him by reading His word daily.

Then, you will read the explanations and bedtime prayers to help you relax in His presence before going to sleep every night. Reading it at night by yourself or with your parents is best. You will understand His never-ending love, care, and devotion towards you as His beloved daughter.

This devotional book will help you lean on Jesus during tough times and teach you how to thank Him during the great times.

Instead of shrinking back in fear over not getting good grades, making new friends, and learning new subjects, you can learn to develop the sense of calmness that God is always with you.

DAY 1: GOD IS ALWAYS WITH YOU

Scripture:
"...for the Lord your God is with you wherever you go."

Joshua 1:9 ESV

Explanation:
Have you ever heard God is with you wherever you go? The Bible proves that He is with you many times over. Sometimes, it's hard to trust that He is always there for and with you, no matter where I go. Whenever you go through hard times, you can take comfort in knowing that He has always been with you, is always with you, and will always be with you no matter what happens.

Bedtime Prayer:

Dear God, thank you for reminding me you're always with me. Amen.

DAY 2: GOD IS FOR YOU

Scripture:
"If God is for us, who can be against us?"

Romans 8:31 ESV

Explanation:
Have you ever had a friend walk away from you out of nowhere? Or had one of your siblings hurt you with their words? If so, you're not the only one hurt by someone you trusted. The good news is that it doesn't matter who is against you in your life. Do you know why? It's because God is for you, and when He is for you, no one can stand against you because He loves you as His precious child.

Bedtime Prayer:

Dear God, please help me remember that you will always be for me, no matter who might be against me. Amen.

DAY 3: HONORING YOUR PARENTS

Scripture:
"Honor your father and your mother, that your days may be long in the land that the Lord your God is giving you."

Exodus 20:12 ESV

Explanation:
When you're young, you sometimes struggle to honor your parents and do what they tell you. But the Bible tells you to honor them because when you do that, you honor them and God, your heavenly father. God wants you to live a long and happy life, and honoring your parents and God can help you achieve that. Even though honoring them can be challenging, you can ask God to help you obey them in all you say and do.

Bedtime Prayer:

Dear God, please help me to honor my parents and you in everything I say and do. Amen.

DAY 4: OBEY YOUR PARENTS

Scripture:
"Children, obey your parents in everything, for this pleases the Lord."

Colossians 3:20 ESV

Explanation:
You may not think that obeying your parents is always the right thing to do. But it is the right thing to do because it pleases them and the Lord. So the next time your parents ask you to clean your room, set the table, take out the trash, or wash the kitchen table, do it without complaining. Obeying your parents not only makes them happy, but it also makes God smile. I want to make both my parents and God happy.

Bedtime Prayer:

Dear God, please help me remember to obey my parents because it pleases you. Amen.

DAY 5: GOD'S GUIDANCE

Scripture:

"Make me to know your ways, O Lord; teach me your paths."

Psalm 25:4 ESV

Explanation:

You can always turn to God whenever you don't know what to do. When you ask Him to guide you through praying, He will guide you down the right path. Amazingly, I can be brave enough to ask God for guidance at any time. I can ask Him to guide me down the path He wants me to go in school, at home, and throughout every phase of my life.

Bedtime Prayer:

Dear God, please make your ways known to me daily. Amen.

DAY 6: SEEK GOD'S PRESENCE

Scripture:

"Seek the Lord and his strength; seek his presence continually!"

1 Chronicles 16:11 ESV

Explanation:

You might wonder how you can continually seek God, His presence, and His strength. The answer is very simple. You can seek God daily by praying, reading the Bible, and asking Him to guide you. You can continually seek His presence by calling on Him in good and bad times. He will give you His never-ending guidance and strength throughout your life. You can even teach your friends and family how to seek Him daily by praying for and with them.

Bedtime Prayer:

Dear God, please help me to seek you every day of my life. Amen.

DAY 7: CONFUSION

Scripture:

"For God is not a God of confusion but of peace."

1 Corinthians 14:33 ESV

Explanation:

There will be many days when you are confused. You will be confused by your math homework and unsure why friend-ships are falling apart. God is not the one who is giving you that sort of confusion. That's your mind playing tricks on you. It's making you question what God has done for you. But God is not allowing you to struggle to hurt you. He is doing it to strengthen your faith and reliance on Him. He is not a God of confusion but the God of peace.

Bedtime Prayer:

Dear God, please help me remember that you are the God of peace. Amen.

DAY 8: PEACE

Scripture:

"Peace, I leave with you; my peace I give to you."

John 14:27 ESV

Explanation:

Did you know that God's peace is already inside you? You have access to His peace at any time. But you can often forget that when life distracts you. He is waiting for you to activate it through prayer and calling upon His name. His peace is eternal instead of only temporary. He gives you His peace freely through your faith and saves you through your gift of salvation.

Bedtime Prayer:

Dear God, thank you for always giving me your peace. Amen.

DAY 9: GOD'S FREEDOM

Scripture:
"And you will know the truth, and the truth will set you free."

John 8:32 ESV

Explanation:
You may have learned that you were given freedom by being born in this country. In the U.S., you have many freedoms that others in other countries take for granted. However, the most critical freedom you will ever have is the freedom you have through knowing Jesus as your Lord and Savior. His freedom is the only one that gives you eternal life in heaven. When you know that He died on the cross for your sins, you'll know the truth, and the truth will set you free.

Bedtime Prayer:

Dear God, please help me recognize your truth. Let your truth set me free. Amen.

DAY 10: THE HOLY SPIRIT'S FREEDOM

Scripture:
"... Where the Spirit of the Lord is, there is freedom."

2 Corinthians 3:17 ESV

Explanation:
When you stand up for your faith, you will feel an ultimate sense of peace in your soul, heart, and mind. Where God is, there is always freedom. Where His spirit is, there is a never-ending feeling of peace and freedom. So, no matter what happens in your life, do your best to stand up for your faith. You will feel proud of yourself knowing you followed God's leading. Whenever you are struggling, you can get free from that struggle by praying at any time.

Bedtime Prayer:

Dear God, please help me embrace you through prayer. Please give me your freedom. Amen.

DAY 11: FREE INDEED

Scripture:
"So if the Son sets you free, you will be free indeed."

John 8:36 ESV

Explanation:
You can be free from anything or anyone that might be causing you emotional, mental, spiritual, and physical pain. All you have to do is call on Jesus, and He will set you free. He is the only one who can truly free you from the pain you feel throughout life. Jesus loves you enough that He died for you on the cross to take away your sins. If He sets you free, you are truly free indeed.

Bedtime Prayer:

Dear God, thank you for setting me free by your death on the cross. Amen.

DAY 12: YOU'RE GOD'S CHILD

Scripture:
"...because Christ Jesus has made me his own."

Philippians 3:12 ESV

Explanation:
If you've ever felt let down by your parents, remember God won't ever let you down. Even though you have the earthly parents God gave you, you must remember that you are God's child, first and foremost. You are His holy and precious daughter whom He loves more than you can possibly imagine. No one, not even your earthly mom or dad, can love you the way Jesus loves you. Jesus made you perfect in His image and made you His own through your salvation and your faith.

Bedtime Prayer:

Dear God, thanks for making me your own and accepting me as your child. Amen.

DAY 13: LIVE IN PEACE

Scripture:
"Strive for peace with everyone..."

Hebrews 12:14 ESV

Explanation:
Living in peace with your friends and family can some-times be challenging, but you must try to be at peace with everyone you interact with daily. Instead of getting angry when someone says something mean, you can say that you forgive them. When a friend abandons you, you can still be nice to them; it helps you feel better, and God also smiles at you when you do your best to be at peace with everyone.

Bedtime Prayer:

Dear God, please help me to be at peace with everyone I en-counter daily. Amen.

DAY 14: PEACE AT ALL TIMES

Scripture:
"Now may the Lord of peace himself give you peace at all times in every way."

2 Thessalonians 3:16 ESV

Explanation:
Sometimes, it can feel like your mind and world are in tur-moil. But the good news is, there is a cure for those feelings in your mind. God is always ready, willing, and available to give you His much-needed peace. He is prepared to provide you with His peace at any time, day or night, and He will give you peace whenever you ask Him to, no matter where you are. He will give you peace at all times in every way.

Bedtime Prayer:

Dear God, please help me to accept your peace whenever I need it. Amen.

DAY 15: ANXIETY HAS NO PLACE

Scripture:
"Do not be anxious about anything..."

Philippians 4:6 ESV

Explanation:
Sometimes, it can be hard not to have anxiety about your life, your friendships, schoolwork, or homework. But Jesus can help you not to have any anxiety. He tells you not to be anxious about anything. I can give my anxiety up to Him and ask Him to carry everything I'm anxious about instead of having it weigh me down. I'm very thankful that through my faith and trust in Jesus, anxiety has no place in my life. Because of Jesus, I don't have to let anxiety control me.

Bedtime Prayer:

Dear God, thank you for telling me not to worry about anything. Amen.

DAY 16: NOT AFRAID OF THE DARK

Scripture:
"In peace, I will lie down and sleep; for you alone, O Lord, make me dwell in safety."

Psalm 4:8 ESV

Explanation:
It's normal to be afraid of the dark. But the good news is you don't have to be scared of the dark. God wants you to lie down and sleep in peace because He is always watching over you and keeping you safe. I can declare His promises each time I feel afraid of the dark. He is watching over me and helping me dwell in safety. Because of my faith, I no longer have to fear the dark. What a relief!

Bedtime Prayer:

Dear God, thank you for saying that I don't need to be afraid of the dark. Amen.

DAY 17: LIVE IN PEACE WITH EVERYONE

Scripture:
"If possible, so far as it depends on you, live peaceably with all."

Romans 12:18 ESV

Explanation:
Sometimes, you may want to tell one of your friends at school everything on your mind. But it is better to remain calm and peaceful than always to speak your mind. Jesus says that it is up to you to live in peace with everyone around you. That means remaining calm no matter who or what upsets you. Instead of saying how you feel, ask God for His help to keep yourself calm and quiet. There is no point in ever starting fights or arguments.

Bedtime Prayer:

Dear God, please help me live peacefully with everyone I know. Amen.

DAY 18: BLESSED ARE THE PEACEMAKERS

Scripture:
"Blessed are the peacemakers..."

Mathew 5:9 ESV

Explanation:
If you've ever seen two friends fighting on the playground at school, have you ever tried to break up the fight between them? Whenever you try to get your friends to stop fighting, you do what Jesus did on earth—being a peacemaker. When you're a peacemaker, you'll be blessed because you're helping others realize their friendship is more important than who is right or wrong. I can help classmates restore their friendships with each other instead of letting a war of words come between them.

Bedtime Prayer:

Dear God, please help me to be a peacemaker like you were. Amen.

DAY 19: YOU'RE GOD'S FRIEND

Scripture:

"...but I have called you friends, for all that I have heard from my Father I have made known to you."

John 15:15 ESV

Explanation:

It can be hard to make friends in school. But there is a true friend that will never let you down. That's Jesus. He has called you His friend since He formed you and made you. Everything that God made Jesus aware of, He will help you understand it throughout your life, too. I'm honored to be Jesus' friend. He is the most important friend I have in life. I know He will reveal what I need to know in His timing.

Bedtime Prayer:

Dear God, thank you for being my most faithful friend. Amen.

DAY 20: FRIENDSHIP WITH GOD

Scripture:

"The friendship of the Lord is for those who fear him, and he makes known to them his covenant."

Psalm 25:14 ESV

Explanation:

When someone tells you to "fear the Lord," it doesn't mean to be afraid or even terrified of Him. Instead, it means to have a healthy and honorable respect for Him as the ultimate authority figure in your life. He can and will give you the knowledge that you need to succeed. All you have to do is ask Him to reveal things to you. You're part of His holy covenant as His friend. I want to fear, love, and respect God too.

Bedtime Prayer:

Dear God, please help me know, love, fear, and respect you daily. Amen.

DAY 21: SELFISHNESS

Scripture:
"Let each of you look not only to his own interests but also to the interests of others."

Philippians 2:4 ESV

Explanation:
It is very important to consider the interests of your family, friends, classmates, and teachers. God wants you to be selfless instead of selfish and only think of yourself, your wants, and your needs. Ask God to help you see the needs of others around you. Pray and ask Him to reveal to you how you can help others and be a witness to them. You could end up changing someone's life.

Bedtime Prayer:
Dear God, please teach me to see others' needs instead of mine. Amen.

DAY 22: GREATER LOVE

Scripture:
"Greater love has no one than this, that someone lay down his life for his friends."

John 15:13 ESV

Explanation:
It can be intimidating and scary to hear this verse about laying down your life for your friends. Hopefully, you will never have to die for your friends. But the good news is that Jesus already laid down His life on the cross to take away your sins. Jesus' love is the most fantastic love you can ever experience. His love is the greatest love of all. It can never be replicated or taken away from you.

Bedtime Prayer:
Dear God, thank you for showing me the greatest love of all time. Amen.

DAY 23: ASK FOR WHAT YOU NEED

Scripture:
"And my God will supply every need of yours..."

Philippians 4:19 ESV

Explanation:
When you ask your siblings or parents for the things you need in your daily life, you can ask God for the things you need, too, such as strength, determination, love, strength, and kindness toward others. God always provides for your basic needs, like food and water, and for your spiritual needs, like strengthening your faith through prayer and worship. He provides for you through schooling, keeps you safe from harm, and helps you provide for others' needs.

Bedtime Prayer:

Dear God, thanks for providing for me every day. Amen.

DAY 24: ASK IN HIS NAME

Scripture:
"...If you ask me anything in my name, I will do it."

John 14:13-14 ESV

Explanation:
You don't have to be afraid to ask God for anything. This verse reminds you that He will do it for you whatever you ask for in Jesus' name. If you need an A on a test, ask Him to help you study hard to get that A. If you need a miracle for your health or a family member's health, He will grant it if it's His will. So ask for anything and everything in His name.

Bedtime Prayer:

Dear God, please help me be brave and bold enough to ask for anything in your name. Amen.

DAY 25: YOU CAN DO ALL THINGS

Scripture:
"I can do all things through him who strengthens me..."

Philippians 4:13 ESV

Explanation:
Do you fully believe you can do everything through Christ? You honestly can do everything through Christ who strengthens you. He strengthens you every day for your life's battles. He equips you to overcome every obstacle that school, life, and friends throw at you. You can and will get through every obstacle with His help. There is nothing that you can't do with God at your side and His strength within you. Declare, "I can do all things through Him who gives me strength."

Bedtime Prayer:

Dear God, please help me believe that I can do everything through you. Amen.

DAY 26: APART FROM ME

Scripture:
"...apart from me, you can do nothing."

John 15:5 ESV

Explanation:
You might be wondering if it's true that you can't do anything apart from God. But it's true. Whenever you try to do things without God and in your strength, you'll unfortunately lose every time. But when you put your first trust in God, you will win in every situation, get good grades in school, pass challenging tests, be close with your family, make great Godly friends, and help make a difference by leading others to Christ through your words and actions.

Bedtime Prayer:

Dear God, thank you for reminding me that I can't do anything without you. Amen.

DAY 27: WORK FOR GOD

Scripture:
"Whatever you do, work heartily, as for the Lord and not for men…"

Colossians 3:23-24 ESV

Explanation:
When you get up in the morning, is your first thought, "Great. How will I get through my chores or my schoolwork today?" You're not the only one who has felt like that. But whenever you do a chore, your schoolwork, your homework, or even take your dog for a walk, remember that you're doing everything for the glory of God. Ask Him to help you change your attitude and heart about your daily activities.

Bedtime Prayer:

Dear God, please help me to do everything because I'm doing it for you. Amen.

DAY 28: ALL FOR GOD

Scripture:
"So, whether you eat or drink, or whatever you do, do all to the glory of God."

1 Corinthians 10:31 ESV

Explanation:
No matter what subject you do, whether it's reading, writing, math, science, or history, you can study those subjects with a good attitude. You even do that whenever you eat dinner or sip your favorite drink for God's glory. Whenever your parents or grandparents ask you to clean your room, set the table, or do laundry, you can remind yourself that you're doing all those things for God's glory. Ask God to help you remember that you are doing things for Him and Him alone.

Bedtime Prayer:

Dear God, help me to do everything for your glory. Amen.

DAY 29: ENJOY SCHOOL

Scripture:
"Keep hold of instruction; do not let go; guard her, for she is your life."

Proverbs 4:13 ESV

Explanation:
It can be hard to stay focused in school every day, especially when you struggle with certain subjects. But listening to your teachers' instructions is important because everything you learn will help you as you grow up. What you learn in school can help you make the right choices later in life. The most important thing to do is remember God's instructions. Staying close to Him will help you learn hard lessons, strengthening your relationship with Him.

Bedtime Prayer:
Dear God, please help me enjoy attending school daily. Amen.

DAY 30: LEARN DIFFERENT SKILLS IN SCHOOL

Scripture:
"As for these four youths, God gave them learning and skill in all literature and wisdom..."

Daniel 1:17 ESV

Explanation:
What is your favorite subject to learn in school? What is your least favorite or most challenging subject to learn? Whenever you struggle to learn math, English, reading, writing, or science, ask God to help you understand it. He will give you an understanding of the subjects you're struggling with at the right time. He will never let you down. Ask God to provide you with the wisdom to pass your classes easily. Ask Him to help you understand what He is trying to teach you every day.

Bedtime Prayer:
Dear God, please help me never to stop learning new skills. Amen.

DAY 31: DOING THE RIGHT THING (PART 1)

Scripture:

"To do righteousness and justice is more acceptable to the Lord than sacrifice."

Proverbs 21:3 ESV

Explanation:

It can be hard to figure out what is good, right, and just in life. Don't be afraid to ask your parents whenever you aren't sure what is right, good, and just. Most importantly, ask God what the good, right, and just things are. Ask Him what good, right, and just things you can do to make this world a much better place. These things can be opening the door for someone, cooking a meal for your elderly neighbor, or helping your dad shovel the snow. God will guide you.

Bedtime Prayer:

Dear God, please help me to do what's right and just in your eyes. Amen.

DAY 32: DOING THE RIGHT THING (PART 2)

Scripture:

"So whoever knows the right thing to do and fails to do it, for him it is sin."

James 4:17 ESV

Explanation:

You sin whenever you know the right thing to do and still don't do it. Don't worry. Everyone sins daily. But whenever you sin, you can automatically ask for forgiveness for the things that you have done. Ask God to help you know the right thing to do every day. Ask Him how you can do the right things for the good and glory of His name, and He will answer you and guide you.

Bedtime Prayer:

Dear God, please help me always do my best to do the right thing. Amen.

DAY 33: PAY ATTENTION

Scripture:
"Therefore, we must pay much closer attention to what we have heard, lest we drift away from it."

Hebrews 2:1 ESV

Explanation:
Do you read the Bible every day? It can help you understand more about who God is and what He has done for you. Just like you read the materials in school to be better prepared for your school tests, reading the Bible daily helps you get closer to God. He wants you to see Him for who He really is. He wants you to pay attention to what He tells you daily, so you don't drift away from your knowledge of knowing Him as your Lord and Savior.

Bedtime Prayer:
Dear God, teach me to pay more attention to what you tell me daily. Amen

DAY 34: BETTER DAYS ARE COMING

Scripture:
"For I consider that the sufferings of this present time are not worth comparing with the glory that is to be revealed to us."

Romans 8:18 ESV

Explanation:
Whenever you go through tough times, remember that god said they wouldn't last forever. There are better times ahead in your life on earth. Better times are coming when you get to heaven. Just think, your beast days on earth haven't yet been experienced. When you get to heaven, you will be praising your Lord and Savior Jesus Christ forever. The pain that you're going through on earth can't even compare to what glories await you in heaven one day.

Bedtime Prayer:
Dear God, please remind me that better days are coming soon. Amen.

DAY 35: HOW GOOD GOD IS (PART 1)

Scripture:
"For God so loved the world, that he gave his only Son, that whoever believes in him should not perish but have eternal life."

John 3:16 ESV

Explanation:
God loves you even more than your parents do. He sent His one and only Son, Jesus Christ, to save you and the rest of the world from sin and death. He died for you so you can have freedom from sin and establish a deep relationship with Him. Even though you sin daily, Jesus saw you as worthy and put all your sins upon Himself on the cross. He saved you so you can be in heaven with Him forever. That's how perfect God is.

Bedtime Prayer:

Dear God, thank you for sending Jesus to save me! Amen.

DAY 36: HOW GOOD GOD IS (PART 2)

Scripture:
"I believe that I shall look upon the goodness of the Lord in the land of the living!"

Psalm 27:13 ESV

Explanation:
Whether you notice Him or not, the goodness of God is all around you every single day. The beauty of a sunrise as you go to school, the smell of the air right after a rainstorm, being able to hug your family members or pet after a long day at school, seeing your family member or friend come through a difficult illness with no permanent side effects, and passing a difficult test are all instances when you see the goodness of God in and over your life.

Bedtime Prayer:

Dear God, please help me see your goodness every day of my life. Amen.

DAY 37: HOW GOOD GOD IS PART 3

Scripture:

And we know that for those who love God, all things work together for good..."

Romans 8:28 ESV

Explanation:

God works everything together for His good and His glory. He called you to be a witness to Him in everything you say and do. When you face difficult times, it may seem that God has forgotten about you, and you might be tempted to think He has stopped working everything out in your life for His glory and good. Just pray and ask Him to reveal how good, excellent, and glorious He is. He will reveal His wonderful plan in His timing and His ways.

Bedtime Prayer:

Dear God, thank you for working together on everything for my good. Amen.

DAY 38: TASTE AND SEE

Scripture:

"Oh, taste and see that the Lord is good!"

Psalm 34:8 ESV

Explanation:

Whenever you taste your favorite drink or food, you're tasting and seeing that God has always been, is being, and will always be good to you. When your parents cook you a great meal after a difficult day at school, or when your grandparents spoil you by making your favorite meal for your birthday, along with cake and ice cream, it makes you realize how loved you are not just by your family or grandparents. You're even more loved by God. He has, is, and always will be good.

Bedtime Prayer:

Dear God, please help me to taste and see your goodness daily. Amen.

DAY 39: EVERY PERFECT GIFT

Scripture:
"Every good gift and every perfect gift is from above..."

James 1:17 ESV

Explanation:
Waking up every day after getting a good night's sleep is a gift from God. Getting a good night's sleep is from God. Having a place to sleep, an animal to pet and cuddle, food to eat, and water to drink are all great gifts from Him. But knowing Jesus as your Lord and Savior is the greatest gift that God can and will ever give you. Everything that you have is a gift from Him.

Bedtime Prayer:

Dear God, help me show everyone that all we have are gifts from you. Amen.

DAY 40: DON'T JUDGE

Scripture:
"Judge not, and you will not be judged;"

Luke 6:37 ESV

Explanation:
You've probably heard this saying from God: Don't judge, and then you won't be judged. You don't want people judging you for how you act, talk, walk, look, or sing. You don't want to be judged by the unique talents that God gave you. You may not always realize that you're judging someone until after the fact. Ask God to help you know when you're about to judge a schoolmate, friend, or teacher. You don't want any of them judging you, so do your best not to judge them.

Bedtime Prayer:

Dear God, please help me not to judge anyone. Amen.

DAY 41: DON'T CONDEMN

Scripture:
"...condemn not, and you will not be condemned;"

Luke 6:37 ESV

Explanation:
You don't like it when people condemn you, right? That's how your friends feel when you condemn them for how they talk, read, or write. You don't like it when people condemn you. So why would you condemn someone? It says in the Bible not to condemn anyone else unless you want to be condemned. So, the next time you think of condemning one of your friends, remember that you could be condemned in the same way by them if you don't keep your thoughts to yourself.

Bedtime Prayer:

Dear God, please help me not to condemn others in any way. Amen.

DAY 42: FORGIVENESS

Scripture:
"...forgive, and you will be forgiven."

Luke 6:37 ESV

Explanation:
Forgiveness is one of the most important things you'll ever learn. You may not want to forgive people who have hurt you, but God will make a way for you to forgive them. Forgiveness helps you be set free from constantly thinking about the pain the person caused you. It also frees you from holding grudges against them for the rest of your life. It helps you move on and continue with your life. Forgiveness may help you rekindle the relationship you thought you'd lost.

Bedtime Prayer:

Dear God, please help me to forgive the way you forgive me daily. Amen.

DAY 43: DON'T JUDGE BY APPEARANCES

Scripture:
"Do not judge by appearances, but judge with right judgment."

John 7:24 ESV

Explanation:
God tells you never to judge someone you love or even someone you don't know based on their appearance. He wants you to judge them correctly as God looks at them: by their faith. Ask yourself how you can help them improve their lives and relationship with God instead of judging them by their appearance when they come to school, sports practice, or in any situation. God doesn't judge you by your appearance. He looks at your inner heart, so do the same for others.

Bedtime Prayer:

Dear God, please help me not to judge anyone by how they look. Amen.

DAY 44: REJOICE WITH THOSE WHO REJOICE

Scripture:
"Rejoice with those who rejoice, weep with those who weep."

Romans 12:15 ESV

Explanation:
Whenever one of your friends gets a new gadget you want, it can be hard not to judge them. You'll want to be jealous and think, "How come they got another new toy? Why can't I ever get a new toy?" This verse teaches you to rejoice with your friends when they get a new toy instead of being jealous. This verse also teaches you to be sad and cry with them when they cry. Just let them know that you're there for them.

Bedtime Prayer:

Dear God, please help me to rejoice whenever my friends and family rejoice. Amen.

DAY 45: LIVE IN HARMONY WITH OTHERS

Scripture:
"Live in harmony with one another."

Romans 12:15-16 ESV

Explanation:
Living in harmony with your siblings isn't always easy. They will always annoy you at some point or another, not just when you're a little kid. As you get older, they will annoy you even more. He wants you to do your best to live in harmony with them now because it prepares you to get along with them later in life. If you get along with your siblings now, you'll most likely get along with them when you're older. God smiles when you live in harmony with your siblings.

Bedtime Prayer:

Dear God, please teach me how to live in harmony with my siblings. Amen

DAY 46: DON'T THINK TOO HIGHLY OF YOURSELF

Scripture:

"Never be wise in your own sight."

Romans 12:15-16 ESV

Explanation:

There will be times when you might think of yourself as a better athlete, reader, instrument player, or singer than your friends, family members, or classmates. But whenever those thoughts come into your mind, you can tell yourself that it is better to be humble than to think too highly of yourself. The last thing you'd want is someone coming down on you for the way you think too highly of yourself. God wants you to be humble instead of being full of yourself.

Bedtime Prayer:

Dear God, please help me never to think I'm better than any-one else. Amen.

DAY 47: THINK OF OTHERS

Scripture:
"Let no one seek his own good but the good of his neighbor."

1 Corinthians 10:24 ESV

Explanation:
There will be times when you'll only think of yourself, which is why you aren't perfect. No one is perfect except Jesus. He doesn't condemn you for not being perfect. Learning to seek out the interests of others and asking what they need is a great idea instead of just thinking of yourself all of the time. Thinking of others instead of yourself helps you eliminate your selfishness. This world and everyone in it isn't and never will be all about you at any time.

Bedtime Prayer:

Dear God, please help me to think of others before thinking of myself. Amen.

DAY 48: BE HUMBLE (PART 1)

Scripture:
"Do nothing from selfish ambition or conceit, but in humility count others more significant than yourselves."

Philippians 2:3 ESV

Explanation:
Take a second and look back. When was the last time you were intentionally or unintentionally selfish? But God warns you in this verse not to do anything out of selfish ambition. Having selfish ambition means you only think of yourself instead of thinking about how your choices will hurt or benefit those around you. Instead of being selfish, God wants you to be humble and consider others more important than you are. Think of them instead of thinking of yourself.

Bedtime Prayer:

Dear God, help me to think of others before thinking of myself. Amen.

DAY 49: BE HUMBLE (PART 2)

Scripture:
"With all humility and gentleness, with patience, bearing with one another in love..."

Ephesians 4:2 ESV

Explanation:
Instead of being self-centered and only thinking of yourself, you have to start looking toward the interests of others in your everyday life. When you train your body, mind, and spirit to think of others instead of yourself, you learn to show gentleness and patience and bear everything with your friends, family, and even those you just met in love. God smiles upon you when you help others and think of others before thinking of yourself. Be gentle and patient and bear with one another in love.

Bedtime Prayer:

Dear God, help me to be humble, patient, and loving to everyone. Amen.

DAY 50: DON'T COMPARE YOURSELF

Scripture:
"Having gifts that differ according to the grace given to us, let us use them..."

Romans 12:6 ESV

Explanation:
It can be hard not to compare yourself to others. Instead of looking down on yourself for your voice, way of thinking, or abilities, God wants you to enjoy your uniqueness. He wants you to love your uniqueness. He wants you to acknowledge the gifts that He gave you as true gifts from Him. He is the one who made you with unique gifts and talents. Instead of comparing yourself, ask Him how you can use your unique talents to make the world a better place every day.

Bedtime Prayer:

Dear God, please help me to stop comparing myself to others. Amen.

DAY 51: LEAD OTHERS TO CHRIST (PART 1)

Scripture:
"And they said, "Believe in the Lord Jesus, and you will be saved, you and your household."

Acts 16:31 ESV

Explanation:
Here are simple tips if you want to lead others to Christ but aren't sure how to do it. You can help lead others to Christ by praying for and with them. Invite them to church. Walk with them and be there for them, just like Jesus was. You can help them believe in Jesus by leading them in prayer: "Lord, I know I'm a sinner. Please forgive my sins. Come into my heart. I make you my Lord and Savior from this day forward. Amen."

Bedtime Prayer:

Dear God, help me to lead others to You through my words and actions. Amen.

DAY 52: LEAD OTHERS TO CHRIST (PART 2)

Scripture:
"Go into all the world and proclaim the gospel to the whole creation."

Mark 16:15 ESV

Explanation:
This verse can be confusing to you. But it doesn't mean you must go everywhere to proclaim the gospel. Instead, God wants you to proclaim His goodness, grace, love, and mercy no matter where you go. It doesn't matter to Him whether you're in school, at home, on the sports team, on a vacation to Florida, or even on a mission trip in another country. Whenever and wherever you proclaim the Gospel, God smiles at you because you tell others how much He loves them.

Bedtime Prayer:

Dear God, please help me to proclaim Your Gospel everywhere I go. Amen.

DAY 53: EXCEPT THROUGH JESUS

Scripture:

"I am the way, and the truth, and the life. No one comes to the Father except through me."

John 14:6 ESV

Explanation:

Many people will try to convince you there are many ways to get to heaven. Some of these ways include but aren't limited to trying to convince you that another religion besides Christianity leads you to get to heaven or worshiping a god besides the one true God. Remember, there is only one way to reach Heaven: knowing Jesus as your Savior. No one comes to the Father except through knowing Jesus first.

Bedtime Prayer:

Dear God, help me tell others the only way to heaven is through knowing Jesus. Amen.

DAY 54: FORGIVE THEM 77, NOT 7 TIMES

Scripture:

"I do not say to you seven times, but seventy-seven times..."

Mathew 21:18-19 ESV

Explanation:

Have you ever wondered how often you are supposed to forgive someone who has hurt you? Peter, one of the disciples, asked Jesus how many times he should forgive someone, and Jesus said not only to forgive the person who hurt you seven times but seventy-seven times. So that's 149 times or more per person whenever someone hurts you. That might seem like a lot, but Jesus forgives you every day. So, how can you not forgive others when they hurt you?

Bedtime Prayer:

Dear God, help me forgive others the same number of times you forgive me. Amen.

DAY 55: SHINE YOUR LIGHT

Scripture:
"In the same way, let your light shine before others..."

Mathew 5:14-16 ESV

Explanation:
You might wonder what you can do to shine your light among your classmates, teachers, friends, family, and everyone you know. But here are some quick tips: smile, be there for others who are struggling, help others by opening doors for people, worship with your family and friends, tell others about Jesus every chance you get, pray for people and with them. Tell them how Jesus has saved and impacted your life. Be Jesus' hands and feet through your words and actions.

Bedtime Prayer:
Dear God, please help my light shine through my words and actions. Amen.

DAY 56: HUMBLENESS TAKES YOU FURTHER IN LIFE

Scripture:
"Whoever humbles himself like this child is the greatest in the kingdom of heaven."

Mathew 18:4 ESV

Explanation:
Being humble is a great trait to master from a young age. Ask Him to teach you to be humble instead of thinking you are more important or better than someone else. The more humble you can be, the further you'll go, and the better off you'll be. You will learn to help others without expecting anything from them in return. Remember, God helps you out of the goodness of His heart, so how can you not be as humble as Him every day?

Bedtime Prayer:
Dear God, help me stay humble throughout my life. Amen.

DAY 57: DON'T TALK BAD ABOUT YOUR NEIGHBOR

Scripture:

"You shall not bear false witness against your neighbor."

Exodus 20:16 ESV

Explanation:

Bearing false witness against your neighbor sounds complicated. So, let's simplify it for you. It means hurting someone's pride or reputation by saying mean things about them, their friends, and family and starting rumors about them. It also includes spreading lies that harm them mentally, physically, spiritually, and emotionally. God doesn't want you to talk badly about your neighbor, schoolmate, friend, family, or anyone you know. He wants you to show everyone His love. Don't talk bad about anyone because you wouldn't like it if someone talked bad about you.

Bedtime Prayer:

Dear God, please help me not to talk badly about anyone I meet. Amen.

DAY 58: LOVE ONE ANOTHER

Scripture:

"By this, all people will know that you are my disciples if you have love for one another."

John 13:35 ESV

Explanation:

Loving one another isn't always easy as a kid. But Jesus has shown you exactly how to love your friends, siblings, classmates, and even bullies you can't stand. Take it from Jesus Himself: He was mocked, ridiculed, and put on the cross to take death as your punishment to make you free and give you salvation. You can show others that you are truly one of Jesus' disciples by being Jesus' hands and feet and by living by Jesus' example by loving them the way Jesus loves you.

Bedtime Prayer:

Dear God, please help me love others as you love me. Amen.

DAY 59: NOT ASHAMED OF THE GOSPEL

Scripture:
"For I am not ashamed of the gospel..."

Romans 1:16 ESV

Explanation:
Have you ever been made fun of for telling others about Jesus? Have you ever been bullied for sharing your faith? You'll realize that people will always look down upon you because they may not understand it. But that gives you the perfect opportunity to explain what your faith and your relationship with Jesus means to you and how He has impacted your life. Tell them that Jesus and reading His word has helped you through hard times. Proudly proclaim that you will never be ashamed of God's word.

Bedtime Prayer:

Dear God, help me to proclaim your good news. I'm never ashamed of you. Amen.

DAY 60: I'M A CHILD OF GOD

Scripture:
"By this, we know that we love the children of God..."

1 John 5:2 ESV

Explanation:
Has someone you trust, like your parents, siblings, or teachers, ever told you that you are a true child of God? How did you react to hearing that astonishing fact? Everyone who loves you, like Jesus loves you, only proves that you are one of God's beloved children. If you ever doubt yourself and your abilities, remember that you're God's daughter and have unique skills and talents that He gave you and only you. Loving others the way God loves you makes you a child of God, too.

Bedtime Prayer:

Dear God, thank you that I'm your beloved child. Amen.

DAY 61: GOD'S PLANS FOR ME

Scripture:
"For I know the plans I have for you, declares the Lord..."

Jeremiah 29:11 ESV

Explanation:
Whenever you feel like you don't know where to go, how to finish a homework assignment, how to start studying for a test, or how to approach a friend about how they hurt your feelings, take heart. Even before things concern you, God knows what you think and worry about. He knew exactly how you'd feel about that test, your friendships, how to do your homework, and where He would lead you throughout your life. He has plans to prosper and help you in every way.

Bedtime Prayer:

Dear God, thanks for establishing beautiful plans for my life before it even began. Amen.

DAY 62: YOUR CITIZENSHIP

Scripture:
"But our citizenship is in heaven, and from it we await a Savior, the Lord Jesus Christ."

Philippians 3:20 ESV

Explanation:
You have been on earth for only a few years, but no one, not even Jesus, knows how many years that is for each person. No one, not even Jesus, knows when God will call you home to your eternity. You are on earth because you are assigned a holy purpose God gave you. He will help you know how to finish your divine assignment and finish your race of bringing people to Christ with love, grace, and dignity. Your true citizenship is in heaven.

Bedtime Prayer:

Dear God, thank you for my true citizenship in heaven with you. Amen.

DAY 63: YOUR HOLY PURPOSE

Scripture:
"The Lord has made everything for its purpose..."

Proverbs 16:4 ESV

Explanation:
You may not believe it, but God created you for His purpose. He made you and every unique talent He gave you so you could bring people to know the goodness of Christ Jesus in your own unique way. So the next time you doubt yourself or your ability to make a difference, ask Him to help you believe in yourself. Believe that with His help and guidance, you find ways to achieve His wonderful purpose for your life.

Bedtime Prayer:

Dear God, please help me find my holy purpose in life with your help. Amen.

DAY 64: FULFILL HIS PURPOSE

Scripture:
"The Lord will fulfill his purpose for me..."

Psalm 138:8 ESV

Explanation:
The next time you feel unqualified to tell people in school, at home, or at practice about how God can make a difference in their lives, remember that God loves it when you tell others about Him. Don't give in to those thoughts negatively that your words can't make any difference. Talk to the people who God leads you to. You could change someone's life for the better just by telling them about Jesus. You could even end up saving someone's life!

Bedtime Prayer:

Dear God, please fulfill your purpose for my life in your timing. Amen.

DAY 65: TAKE COURAGE

Scripture:
"Be strong, and let your heart take courage, all you who wait for the Lord!"

Psalm 31:24 ESV

Explanation:
If there are people who are bullying you at school for any reason, take courage and remember that God is with you. You could be getting bullied for numerous reasons, such as for professing your faith, taking tests outside of the classroom, not making it on the basketball team, because of the way you like to read or the way you look. Instead of "getting even" with them, remember to wait for God to have the last word. He will give you courage amongst your bullies.

Bedtime Prayer:
Dear God, please help me get courage from you daily. Amen.

DAY 66: BE WATCHFUL

Scripture:
"Be watchful, stand firm in the faith..."

1 Corinthians 16:13 ESV

Explanation:
God wants you to be watchful every day. He wants you to be watching for signs of deception from your friends. Remember, anybody you thought you could trust suddenly starts leading you down the dark path that takes you away from Him; that means they are trying to deceive you. You must stand firm in your faith and declare that you follow Jesus, not the worldly path. You know Jesus is the only way to get to heaven.

Bedtime Prayer:
Dear God, please help me stand firm in my faith against deception. Amen.

DAY 67: WAIT FOR THE LORD

Scripture:
"Wait for the Lord; be strong, and let your heart take courage; wait for the Lord!"

Psalm 27:14 ESV

Explanation:
When you're a kid, it's hard to wait. It can be even harder when you've been diagnosed with cancer and are waiting to get better. No matter what you're waiting for, God encourages you to be strong, take heart, and wait for Him. If you're in the hospital seeking cancer treatment, be an encouragement to other kids who don't know Jesus and the freedom and hope He offers them. Offer to pray for them and with them. Ask them if they'd like to invite Jesus into their lives.

Bedtime Prayer:

Dear God, please give me courage while I wait for you to guide me. Amen.

DAY 68: DON'T BE AFRAID

Scripture:
"Even though I walk through the valley of the shadow of death, I will fear no evil..."

Psalm 23:4 ESV

Explanation:
Whenever you are going through challenging times, you might be afraid of the unknown, what lies ahead, what could happen to you, or if you'll pass your math test. But you don't have to be afraid. God wants you to know that even when you walk through your darkest time and even through the valley of the shadow of death, He is always by your side. No matter what or who tries to harm you, they are no match for His grace, love, and mercy.

Bedtime Prayer:

Dear God, please help me never to be afraid because you're with me. Amen.

DAY 69: SPIRIT OF SELF-CONTROL

Scripture:

"For God gave us a spirit not of fear but of power and love and self-control."

2 Timothy 1:7 ESV

Explanation:

When was the last time you wanted to yell at your parents, siblings, or friends? What stopped you from giving them a piece of your mind? The truth is that God stopped you because He gave you a spirit of a sound mind and a spirit of self-control. Self-control means holding yourself back from mouthing off to someone because you realize that it'll do you no good. Plus, once you say something to someone, you can't take it back. You can only apologize.

Bedtime Prayer:

Dear God, please help me control my words and actions. Amen.

DAY 70: RESPECT OTHERS

Scripture:

"Remember your leaders, those who spoke to you the word of God."

Hebrews 13:7 ESV

Explanation:

You may not always agree with those in your life who are in positions of authority. Those people are your parents, older siblings, grandparents, teachers and coaches. God wants you to respect them in every way possible. Your parents, grand-parents, and siblings help teach you about God. So do your teachers and coaches. The most important authority figure is God Himself. He should be loved, honored, and respected the most. He put the right people in your life to teach you about His goodness, mercy, and love.

Bedtime Prayer:

Dear God, please help me respect everyone in authority over me. Amen.

DAY 71: ALL THINGS ARE POSSIBLE

Scripture:
"With man, this is impossible, but with God, all things are possible."

Mathew 19:26 ESV

Explanation:
You may not think you'll be able to make the baseball team, make the cheerleading squad, pass the difficult science test, or beat the sickness that you have. But rest assured, God knows exactly how you feel. With Him, all things are possible. Not just one thing or some things, but all things are possible through Him. He will help you make the team cheer squad and help you pass the science test. He will cure you. He will do all things that seem impossible.

Bedtime Prayer:
Dear God, help me to remember that nothing is impossible through you. Amen.

DAY 72: NOTHING IS TOO HARD FOR GOD

Scripture:
"Is anything too hard for the Lord?"

Genesis 18:14 ESV

Explanation:
While life will be challenging, nothing is too hard for God. The friendship that you thought was beyond repair, God can fix it. God will help you learn the material for the history test you failed to pass the next test. The diagnosis your grandma received: He will help her. God puts troubles in your life to see if you rely on Him or your strength to make it through. Rely on Jesus because nothing is too hard for Him.

Bedtime Prayer:
Dear God, I praise you because there's nothing too difficult for you. Amen.

DAY 73: JESUS NEVER CHANGES

Scripture:
"Jesus Christ is the same yesterday and today and forever."

Hebrews 13:8 ESV

Explanation:
Even though there are people, places, and things that are drastically changing every day, there is one thing that will never change-Jesus' love for you. Nothing will ever make Him love you any more or any less than He loves you right here, right now, in this very moment. Jesus is the only ever-lasting sustenance in your life. He will never change. He is the same today, yesterday, tomorrow, and forever. So, cling to Jesus and His constant presence while your life changes constantly.

Bedtime Prayer:
Dear God, thank you for never changing and being the constant in my life. Amen.

DAY 74: GRACIOUS SPEECH

Scripture:
"Let your speech always be gracious..."

Colossians 4:6 ESV

Explanation:
Whenever you want to give people a piece of your mind, there's that small still very in your head that tells you to reconsider mouthing off. Do you know whose voice that is? That's God talking to you by the power of the Holy Spirit. He wants your words to be gracious. That means speaking kindly instead of being mean. It means willingly helping others even when you don't want to. It means encouraging a friend or family member, even if you're upset. God smiles when you're loving and kind.

Bedtime Prayer:
Dear God, let my words be kind and gracious. Amen.

DAY 75: DON'T BE TROUBLED

Scripture:
"Let not your hearts be troubled. Believe in God; believe also in me."

John 14:1 ESV

Explanation:
A troubled heart can be scary, especially as a kid. You may not understand why you feel the way you do. But you may recognize the uneasiness in the pit of your stomach, the pounding in your chest, and the inability to concentrate in school. All of those things are signs of a troubled heart. But God doesn't want you to have a troubled heart. He wants you to be filled with joy, gladness, and laughter. So believe in Him and trust He will make your heart joyful again.

Bedtime Prayer:
Dear God, help me focus on you, not what my heart and mind tell me. Amen.

DAY 76: TURN THE OTHER CHEEK

Scripture:
"But if anyone slaps you on the right cheek, turn to him the other also."

Mathew 5:38-39 ESV

Explanation:
If you have ever been physically bullied for the way your hair looks, or the way you dress, or called a nerd, it can hurt. But God wants you to turn the other cheek if you've been bul-lied. That doesn't mean you should keep allowing them to abuse you. Instead, it means praying for them, wishing them well, and even telling them God loves them. The kids who bully you might be shocked, but God smiles when you show them His love.

Bedtime Prayer:
Dear God, help me turn the other cheek no matter how peo-ple treat me. Amen.

DAY 77: IMITATE JESUS

Scripture:
"Be imitators of me, as I am of Christ..."

1 Corinthians 11:1 ESV

Explanation:
You might wonder, "How can I be an imitator of Christ at my school, at home, and in my community?" It's simple. You can be like Jesus by being His hands and feet and telling everyone you meet about Him. Spread His love, kindness, goodness, and mercy to kids with no friends. Offer to sit with them at lunch or play with them at recess. Help make a meal for an elderly neighbor. When you imitate Jesus, you impact someone's life for the best.

Bedtime Prayer:

Dear God, help me to imitate you in my thoughts, words, and actions. Amen.

DAY 78: EMBRACE YOUR YOUTH

Scripture:
"Let no one despise you for your youth..."

1 Timothy 4:12 ESV

Explanation:
It can be hard to speak up about your faith and how important it is to you. Many people may not understand why you're so close to Jesus. People may tell you not to bring up Jesus at a young age because no one will listen to you. But that gives you many opportunities to share what Jesus means to you. Don't let anyone talk you out of sharing about the love of Jesus, no matter how young you are. You're never too young to make a difference.

Bedtime Prayer:

Dear God, help me never to be discouraged from telling others about you. Amen.

DAY 79: SET JESUS' EXAMPLE

Scripture:
"...but set the believers an example in speech, in conduct, in love, in faith, in purity."

1 Timothy 4:12 ESV

Explanation:
You might think, "I want to make a difference and set an example for Jesus, but how do I do that?" It's simple. Be loving, kind, caring, and gracious towards everyone you meet daily. Help people without expecting anything from them in return. Pray for people who hurt you and quickly forgive them, just like Jesus. Encourage people who are struggling and lift their spirits. Show love to a classmate who feels left out. However, God wants you to serve and follow His leading.

Bedtime Prayer:

Dear God, please help me to set Jesus' example in everything I say and do. Amen.

DAY 80: TRUST IN GOD

Scripture:
"But I trust in you, O Lord; I say, "You are my God."

Psalm 31:14-15 ESV

Explanation:
Who do you trust in your life? No doubt you trust your parents, siblings, friends, and grandparents. But do you fully trust God? Trusting God can seem like it's tricky. But it's simple. Trusting Him means that you're able to relax when you could be freaking over a test or school project. Trusting Him means knowing that your dad will be ok if he's in the hospital. Trusting Him is knowing He has your back through every situation and feeling His peace that surpasses all understanding.

Bedtime Prayer:

Dear God, please help me to trust in you no matter what happens. Amen.

DAY 81: TRUSTING IN GOD

Scripture:
"When I am afraid, I put my trust in you."

Psalm 56:3 ESV

Explanation:
Being scared is no fun whether you're a full-grown adult
or a kid. No one likes or flat-out choose to be afraid. Scary
things happen all the time in life. But it's what you do in the
face of fear that matters. Instead of cowering away, you can
face whatever scares you head-on and trust that God always
has your back. When you're afraid, trust Him and know that
everything will work out.

Bedtime Prayer:

*Dear God, remind me to trust you whenever I get scared.
Amen.*

DAY 82: KNOWING GOD'S LOVE

Scripture:
*"So we have come to know and to believe the love that God
has for us..."*

1 John 4:16 ESV

Explanation:
You believe that your parents and grandparents love you
with all their hearts, right? Do you know that God loves you
even more than they do? He loves you more than they ever
could. You are His holy, precious child. His daughter. He loves
you so much that He sent His only Son, Jesus, to die for your
sins on the cross so you can have an eternal place with Him
in heaven. His love is unmatched and never-ending. Nothing
you do will ever change His love for you.

Bedtime Prayer:

*Dear God, please help me know your love and teach others
about you. Amen.*

DAY 83: GOD'S LOVE

Scripture:
"...God is love, and whoever abides in love abides in God, and God abides in him."

1 John 4:16 ESV

Explanation:
Showing God's love can look like opening a door for someone coming out of a store, helping your mom fold clothes, or helping your dad set the table. It's cooking a meal for your grandma and spending time with her. It's allowing your little sister to feel better by giving her a much-needed hug when she's had a tough day at school. It's encouraging your friend when she's moving away. It's helping your neighbor shovel snow. It's showing love to everyone in your life.

Bedtime Prayer:

Dear God, help me abide in your love daily. Amen.

DAY 84: REFUGE IN CHRIST

Scripture:
"It is better to take refuge in the Lord than to trust in man."

Psalm 118:8 ESV

Explanation:
You might wonder why trusting God is better than anyone else. The reason is that God can be fully trusted, and everyone on earth can't be fully trusted because everyone has sinned and fallen short of God's glory. But God can never make mistakes. He saved your life by dying on the cross in your place. Your family might be willing to die for you, but Jesus died and rose again for you. Take refuge in Him as your Savior.

Bedtime Prayer:

Dear God, please give me refuge in you daily. Amen.

DAY 85: VERY PRESENT HELP

Scripture:
"God is our refuge and strength, a very present help in trouble."

Psalm 46:1 ESV

Explanation:
Many people, including your parents, friends, teachers, and extended family, can help you in different situations. But only one person can truly help you at a moment's notice. That's Jesus. He is only a second away. Whenever you call on Him, He is there, ready to help you no matter what you're going through or where you might be. It doesn't matter if you're at home, in school or in another country. He is your very present help in times of trouble.

Bedtime Prayer:

Dear God, thank you for being my very present help in tough times. Amen.

DAY 86: GOD WILL ACT

Scripture:
"Commit your way to the Lord; trust in him, and he will act."

Psalm 37:5 ESV

Explanation:
If you have ever had a dream God, put in your heart, rest assured that He can and will help you accomplish it. Instead of trying to achieve your dream on your own, commit your dream to the Lord and continually trust in Him. Even when He seems quiet, He works behind the scenes to help you accomplish your dream. He will act on your behalf in His timing and His ways. Watch how far you'll go with God leading your dream.

Bedtime Prayer:

Dear God, please help me believe you will act in my best interest. Amen.

DAY 87: KEEP HIS COMMANDMENTS

Scripture:
"If you love me, you will keep my commandments."

John 14:15 ESV

Explanation:
Keeping God's commandments is sometimes hard because you sin unintentionally daily. That's because sin is in your life and the world. Sometimes, you may not even realize you sinned until after you said a bad word or something you can't take back. You may be tempted to cheat on a test even though you know it's wrong, or you may want to spread a rumor about someone. If you love God, then you will keep His commandments. Ask for His help and forgiveness, and thank Him for His love.

Bedtime Prayer:
Dear God, please help me keep your commandments. Amen.

DAY 88: ASK GOD ANYTHING

Scripture:
"...if we ask anything according to his will he hears us."

1 John 5:14 ESV

Explanation:
Don't be afraid to ask God anything and everything. You can come before Him any time and ask Him any questions you want. You can tell Him your deepest dreams and desires. If you pray and ask Him anything according to His will, He hears you. He loves it when you talk to Him and spend quality time with Him day or night. So don't be afraid. Go ahead, be bold. Ask Him anything.

Bedtime Prayer:
Dear God, thank you that I can ask you about anything. Amen.

DAY 89: DISCOVER GOD IN HIS WORD

Scripture:
"Whoever gives thought to the word will discover good, and blessed is he who trusts in the Lord."

Proverbs 16:20 ESV

Explanation:
How often are you reading God's word? Every few days, every other day, every few weeks? God knows you get distracted from reading His word by being bombarded with homework, quizzes and tests, and family obligations. But none of those things should ever distract you from wanting to learn more about God in His Word. Ask Him to open your heart to new insight and help you discover new beautiful things about Him every time you open your Bible.

Bedtime Prayer:

Dear God, please help me discover the goodness in your word. Amen.

DAY 90: WALK BY FAITH

Scripture:
"For we walk by faith, not by sight."

2 Corinthians 5:7 ESV

Explanation:
Walking by faith can be challenging because you rely on a God you can't physically see. But when God gets you through tough times, that's when your faith gets stronger. It's when you're going through a tough time, and you can say you trust God instead of falling apart. You fall on your knees, praying instead of falling on your bed crying. You tell yourself, "God's got my back. He's done it before, and He will do it again."

Bedtime Prayer:

Dear God, help me to walk by faith and not by sight. Amen.

DAY 91: I WON'T BE AFRAID

Scripture:
"In God I trust; I shall not be afraid. What can flesh do to me?"

Isaiah 12:2 ESV

Explanation:
Are you bold and brave enough to say that you trust God fully in any situation? Do you believe that He will protect you from all harm? The next time a challenge comes, tell yourself that you can and will conquer it with God's help. If and when you get bullied in school, challenge the bullies by saying, "Bring it on. God's on my side. What can you guys do to me?" Then, see how the bullies respond.

Bedtime Prayer:

Dear God, help me be brave and say, "What can anyone do to me?" Amen.

DAY 92: BE STILL

Scripture:
"Be still, and know that I am God."

Psalm 46:1 ESV

Explanation:
Whenever you go through difficulties with your friends, teachers, siblings, parents, or problems in school, God wants you to be still and know He is God. He already has every solution lined up for you before you ever have the problem you're dealing with. He wants you to rest in His perfect peace and assurance that everything will work out and be ok. He wants you to remember that you don't have to figure everything out because He has already figured everything out for you.

Bedtime Prayer:

Dear God, help me be still and know you're God. Amen.

DAY 93: LOVE IS PATIENT

Scripture:
"Love is patient and kind; love does not envy or boast; it is not arrogant."

1 Corinthians 13:4 ESV

Explanation:
Kids everywhere want to think they are bigger, stronger, faster, smarter, and even richer than the other kids at school. But God doesn't want you to think too highly of yourself like those kids do. He wants you to be gracious, loving, kind, compassionate, and most of all, He wants you to be humble. Being humble is way better than thinking you're better than other people. No one is perfect except Jesus. So be patient, loving, kind, and humble like He wants you to be.

Bedtime Prayer:

Dear God, please help me to be patient, kind, and humble. Amen.

DAY 94: LOVE YOUR ENEMIES

Scripture:
"But love your enemies, and do good, and lend, expecting nothing in return..."

Luke 6:35 ESV

Explanation:
When someone hurts you intentionally, you might automatically think of them as your enemy. You probably won't want anything to do with them anymore. But instead of punishing them, God wants you to love your enemies no matter how they treat you. He wants you to help others and be a servant to them without expecting them to give you anything in return. He wants you to serve others no matter what it may cause you to feel, look, or smell like.

Bedtime Prayer:

Dear God, help me love my enemies no matter how badly they treat me. Amen.

DAY 95: RUTH WAS BLESSED

Scripture:
"May you be blessed by the Lord, my daughter... "

Ruth 3:10 ESV

Explanation:
This Bible story is about a woman named Ruth who wouldn't leave her mother-in-law after her husband died. Naomi, her mother-in-law, saw how loyal she was and wanted her to be blessed by God. Little did she know her prayer would be answered tenfold. Your parents want you to be blessed by God as their daughter, too. They want you to impact the world with your faith, just like Ruth did.

Bedtime Prayer:

Dear God, please help me to be blessed and share your love with others. Amen.

DAY 96: BEING GENEROUS AND KIND

Scripture:
"You have made this last kindness greater than the first..."

Ruth 3:10 ESV

Explanation:
Being kind is much better than being mean to someone. Being kind lets you feel good about yourself, while being mean to someone may make you feel superior to them. God always wants you to have your most recent act of kindness be even better than the first time you were kind to someone. That means no matter how kind you are, you can still strive to be even kinder to people, just like Jesus was. Do your best to be kind and generous every day.

Bedtime Prayer:

Dear God, please help me to be kind and generous to everyone daily. Amen.

DAY 97: ANGEL'S AMONG US

Scripture:
"Do not neglect to show hospitality to strangers, for thereby some have entertained angels unawares."

Hebrews 13:2 ESV

Explanation:
Angels are all around you every day, and you probably aren't even aware of them. They could be keeping you safe from bullies in school, keeping you and your parents from getting into accidents on the road, and protecting you from temptations. They can even be people who you've known your whole life. They don't have to be your grandparent's age. They could be your age too. Treat people kindly because you never know if you speak to an angel.

Bedtime Prayer:

Dear God, help me be kind because I could talk to an angel anytime. Amen.

DAY 98: TAKE EVERY OPPORTUNITY

Scripture:
"...as we have opportunity, let us do good to everyone..."

Galatians 6:10 ESV

Explanation:
When you see an elderly neighbor struggling to cut her grass or shovel her driveway, jump at the opportunity to help her. When your dad asks you to help him carry groceries inside, help him. When your mom needs help watching your baby brother or sister, watch them while she makes dinner. If your younger sister needs help with her science fair project, help her design it. God wants you to jump at every opportunity to help make someone's life easier.

Bedtime Prayer:

Dear God, help me to take all opportunities to help people. Amen.

DAY 99: PURSUE KINDNESS

Scripture:
"Whoever pursues righteousness and kindness will find life, righteousness, and honor."

Proverbs 21:21 ESV

Explanation:
Instead of wanting to be right or to be noticed all of the time, try being humble. It is much better to be humble than to be seen for everything you accomplish. If you're getting noticed for everything you have accomplished, you'll start thinking too much of yourself. God says whoever pursues righteousness and kindness will find life, righteousness, and honor. Just be the nice Christian person God created you to be, not someone who wants to be noticed.

Bedtime Prayer:
Dear God, please teach me to pursue kindness at school and home. Amen.

DAY 100: PERSECUTION OF FAITH

Scripture:
"Blessed are you when others... utter all kinds of evil against you falsely on my account."

Mathew 5:11 ESV

Explanation:
In this broken world, you will be persecuted, looked down upon, and punished for your faith. Yes, it is unfair, but God will bless you when someone mocks you for your faith in Jesus Christ. You will be blessed to follow His ways and lead by His examples even when classmates and friends come down on you, start rumors about you, and call you a know-it-all in school. You will be blessed to follow Him no matter how badly people in school treat you.

Bedtime Prayer:
Dear God, please help me to stand firm among people hurting my faith. Amen.

DAY 101: UNKNOWN FUTURE

Scripture:
"Yet you do not know what tomorrow will bring."

James 4:14 ESV

Explanation:
Even though you never know what each day can bring, embrace each day with the confidence that God is with you no matter what you face. Be patient, loving, and kind to yourself and others. Treat each day as a blessing because every new day you experience is a true gift from God. Whenever you get nervous about the day ahead, turn your worry into prayer and believe He has your back today and in the future. He will never let you down.

Bedtime Prayer:

*Dear God, help me to trust you with my unknown future.
Amen.*

DAY 102: GOD WILL HELP YOU

Scripture:
"...I will strengthen you, I will help you..."

Isaiah 41:10 ESV

Explanation:
Do you ever wonder where your strength comes from? God gives you physical, spiritual, mental, and emotional strength. He equips you with the correct strength when you need it the most. He gives you the physical strength to finish basketball practice despite your exhaustion. He gives you the mental strength to finish studying for your dreaded test. He gives you the emotional strength to forgive when your parents say something hurtful. He gives you the spiritual strength when your faith is shaken.

Bedtime Prayer:

*Dear God, please help me be strong no matter what happens.
Amen.*

DAY 103: HEARING GOD'S WORD

Scripture:
"Now faith is the assurance of things hoped for, the conviction of things not seen."

Hebrews 11:1 ESV

Explanation:
Faith is knowing God is there with you even though you can't see Him. It's feeling His presence in the beating of your heart, the rhythm of the rain, the roar of the ocean, or the rushing of the wind. Faith is knowing that no matter what you've gone through or will go through in the future, God has your back. Faith gives you hope over fear. Faith brings you joy amid suffering. It reassures you the best is yet to come.

Bedtime Prayer:

Dear God, please help me hear your word daily. Amen

DAY 104: TEST OF FAITH

Scripture:
"For you know that the testing of your faith produces steadfastness."

James 1:3 ESV

Explanation:
Sometimes it seems no matter how hard you try, you'll always struggle with math, struggle to make friends, and never have a good relationship with your parents. God doesn't want you to give up on yourself because He never will give up on you. God tests your faith to see if you turn to Him asking for help or try making it yourself. Remember, the testing of your faith produces perseverance. When you persevere, you'll look back and realize that God guided you the entire way.

Bedtime Prayer:

Dear God, please test my faith and help me persevere. Amen.

DAY 105: GOD OF SALVATION

Scripture:
"The Lord is my strength and my song, and he has become my salvation..."

Exodus 15:2 ESV

Explanation:
Have you ever heard your grandma say the Lord is her strength, song, and salvation whenever your family is going through hard times? This verse can be a comfort to you, too. The Lord has been so good to you and has protected you from things that can harm you. No matter your situation, allow Him to be the Lord of your life. Declare that the LORD is your strength and that you'll sing His praises as He strengthens you for your daily battles.

Bedtime Prayer:

Dear God, please help me to keep you as my strength and my salvation. Amen.

DAY 106: GIFT OF GOD

Scripture:
"For by grace you have been saved through faith. And this is not your own doing; it is the gift of God..."

Ephesians 2:8 ESV

Explanation:
There is nothing you can do to make God love you any more or less than the way He loves you right now. You've made it this far only because of His grace, mercy, and love. By grace, you were saved by your faith. You could not do, give, or earn it from God. Grace isn't something you can boast about, either. Instead of bragging about yourself, try bragging about how awesome God is and see how it changes your perspective.

Bedtime Prayer:

Dear God, thank you for saving me with your grace. Amen.

DAY 107: NEVER BEYOND YOUR ABILITY

Scripture:
"...he will not let you be tempted beyond your ability..."

1 Corinthians 10:13 ESV

Explanation:
When a friend tempts you, do you recognize that you're being tempted immediately, or does it take time to figure it out? Ask God whenever you aren't entirely sure of what path to take. God will never let you be tempted beyond what you can bear. He moves on your behalf to help you know the difference between right and wrong. He helps you grow in faith. Thank Him that He never lets you be tempted beyond your ability.

Bedtime Prayer:

Dear God, thank you that I'm never tempted beyond my ability. Amen.

DAY 108: DO NOT ENTER INTO TEMPTATION

Scripture:
"Watch and pray that you may not enter into temptation..."

Mark 14:38 ESV

Explanation:
Whenever you are tempted, it's important to remember that you have a choice. You can either fall into temptation or resist it with God's help. He also gives you the free will to choose whether or not you give in to or resist a temptation. When going through those situations, make sure that you fast and pray for the correct guidance from God. Watch your back, and don't fall into the trap of peer pressure. Ask Him to help you make the right calls throughout life.

Bedtime Prayer:

Dear God, please help me to resist temptation through your strength. Amen.

DAY 109: GOD RESCUES YOU

Scripture:
"Then the Lord knows how to rescue the godly from trials..."

2 Peter 2:9-13 ESV

Explanation:
What has God rescued you from? Has He rescued you from being sick, betrayed by your friends, or bullied at school, or has He allowed you to pass the test you were sure you'd fail? He has rescued you from sin and the power it used to have over you. He forgives you for making mistakes and doesn't hold them against you. He saved you from thinking badly about yourself, too. No matter what happens, He knows how to rescue you from the trials you face.

Bedtime Prayer:

Dear God, thank you for rescuing me from my trials. Amen.

DAY 110: THE UNKNOWN HOUR

Scripture:
"Watch, therefore, for you know neither the day nor the hour."

Mathew 25:13 ESV

Explanation:
It's pretty amazing and wild at the same time that Jesus Himself didn't know the time, day, or the very hour in which He would return on the clouds with fire. You don't know the time, date or hour either. You must do your part and bring as many people as possible to school, home, church, and community to know Christ. Remind yourself to be vigilant and ask for forgiveness. Never be afraid to admit that you're a flawed person.

Bedtime Prayer:

Dear God, help me point others to you even at the unknown hour ahead. Amen.

DAY 111: TRIALS OF VARIOUS KINDS

Scripture:
"Count it all joy, my brothers, when you meet trials of various kinds..."

James 1:2 ESV

Explanation:
You might look at this verse and say, "Wait, how am I supposed to be happy whenever I go through challenges?" This verse means to count every second of your day as a joyful experience because life is what you make of it. If not, you choose to wallow in sadness or anger during a challenging time; that's how you'll feel whenever hard times come. But you'll feel more peace if you train your mind to be relaxed, happy, and joyful when hard times come.

Bedtime Prayer:

Dear God, please help me to rejoice in my trials and pain. Amen.

DAY 112: FATHERS- DON'T PROVOKE

Scripture:
"Fathers, do not provoke your children to anger..."

Ephesians 6:4 ESV

Explanation:
When you were born, your parents were overwhelmed with happiness and fear of the unknown. It takes a lot for your parents to raise you to be the Christian girl they want you to be. They also want you to be a respected Christian woman as an adult. That's why your father has to discipline you. Neither of you likes it. But God doesn't want your dad to make you angry purposefully. If that happens, ask God to help you forgive Him. God will help you repair your relationship.

Bedtime Prayer:

Dear God, please help my dad not to get angry with me. Amen.

DAY 113: BRING CHILDREN UP IN THE LORD

Scripture:
"...but bring them up in the discipline and instruction of the Lord."

Ephesians 6:4 ESV

Explanation:
Whenever your parents have to discipline you, they are showing you the difference between right and wrong. They're bringing you up in the discipline and in the instructions of the Lord. God never disciplines you to punish you, and neither do your parents. They all only want to teach you right from wrong so you can make the right choices both now and when you get older. Wouldn't you rather have people teaching you how to do the right things than be led astray by the world?

Bedtime Prayer:

Dear God, help me to be brought up with your instructions and wisdom. Amen.

DAY 114: FATHERS DON'T DISCOURAGE YOUR CHILDREN

Scripture:
"Fathers, do not provoke your children, lest they become discouraged."

Colossians 3:21 ESV

Explanation:
It can be hard not to get discouraged whenever your dad disciplines you. You might think you'll never be the daughter he wants you to be. But that's the exact opposite of the truth. Your father thinks so highly of you and is so proud of you. Your father can sometimes discourage you even though he doesn't mean to. But forgive him, move on, and let it go instead of holding on to the bitterness. Giving it to God is better than having your self-esteem destroyed by accident.

Bedtime Prayer:

Dear God, help me not to be discouraged by my parents. Amen.

DAY 115: YOUR AWESOME GRANDPARENTS

Scripture:
"Grandchildren are the crown of the aged, and the glory of children is their fathers."

Proverbs 17:6 ESV

Explanation:
There is nothing quite like visiting your grandparents. They truly are some of the most incredible people in the world. They love you so much and think the world of you. They want to shower you with love and enjoy your company. Stay at their house every chance you get. You are the crown of your grandparents. Spend every opportunity you can get to be with them. You never know how long you have with your family. Enjoy every minute you get with your grandparents. Your family is a gift from God.

Bedtime Prayer:
*Dear God, help me to love my parents and grandparents.
Amen.*

DAY 116: CHILDREN ARE A GIFT FROM GOD

Scripture:
"Behold, children are a heritage from the Lord, the fruit of the womb a reward."

Psalm 127:3 ESV

Explanation:
You're a gift from God. You are a gift to your parents and a heritage from God. You are the fruit of your mother's womb and a reward. You're a treasure to your parents. Don't be afraid to come to God or your parents about anything and everything that is bothering you. You're never a mistake. God made you for a beautiful reason, and one of the reasons is to enrich your parent's lives. You can do great things in your life with God's help.

Bedtime Prayer:
*Dear God, thank you that I am a true heritage from you.
Amen.*

DAY 117: WALK IN TRUTH

Scripture:

"I have no greater joy than to hear that my children are walking in the truth. "

3 John 1:4 ESV

Explanation:

Always be proud to walk in the truth of God. There is no greater joy for your parents to know you're walking through your life in God's truth. Proclaim God's goodness throughout your life. Don't be ashamed or afraid to tell others about God. When your parents know you're glorifying God in school, at home, and in life, they see the difference in your life. To know that you're saved brings them so much peace and joy. Be Christ's example and make your parents proud.

Bedtime Prayer:

Dear God, please help my child to follow you throughout their lives. Amen.

DAY 118: DON'T DESPISE CHILDREN

Scripture:

"See that you do not despise one of these little ones..."

Mathew 18:10 ESV

Explanation:

To all the adults in your life, please never discourage or despise the children. It doesn't matter whether you're a teacher, coach, parent, grandparent, uncle, aunt or other extended family member. Never despise one of the children in your care, especially when they are talking about God and His love. Never discourage them from talking about God. God wants you to honor, love, and cherish the kids in your life.

Bedtime Prayer:

Dear God, please help me never to be despised by anyone because of my age. Amen.

DAY 119: TAUGHT BY GOD

Scripture:
"All your children shall be taught by the Lord, and great shall be the peace of your children."

Isaiah 54:13 ESV

Explanation:
Parents, do your best to raise all of your children in the ways and love of the Lord. Allow yourself to be taught by God so you can teach them how to be His example in everything they say and do. When your children are afraid, remind them that God is one prayer away, and He will give them His peace. Teach your children to love and serve others the way Jesus serves you. Teach them to forgive quickly, just as Jesus forgives you. Watch how their peace increases daily.

Bedtime Prayer:

Dear God, help me to always have peace through you. Amen.

DAY 120: DON'T WORSHIP IDOLS

Scripture:
"Little children, keep yourselves from idols."

1 John 5:21 ESV

Explanation:
When you love something more than God, you may unintentionally put things above God. This can include a friend, your dog, a sport you enjoy, a video game you play, or one of your favorite TV shows. If you spend more time doing those activities than with God and reading His word, those are your idols. Ask God to clear your heart of anything you cherish more than your relationship with Him. Ask Him for forgiveness for not putting Him first.

Bedtime Prayer:

Dear God, please help me never to worship idols. Amen

DAY 121: ACT FAITHFULLY

Scripture:

"Lying lips are an abomination to the Lord, but those who act faithfully are his delight."

Proverbs 12:22 ESV

Explanation:

You should always do your best never to lie because that is one thing God hates. Lying lips are an abomination to Him. Lying makes you have to cover your tracks. When you lie, you can start lying all the time. Once one lie gets out, everyone will start having trust issues with you. So, to avoid that, always tell the truth and act faithfully toward God and others. It's always better to tell the truth than to get caught lying. When you act faithfully, God delights in you.

Bedtime Prayer:

Dear God, help me to act faithfully every day. Amen.

DAY 122: DON'T LIE TO ANYONE

Scripture:

"Do not lie to one another..."

Collisions 3:9 ESV

Explanation:

You might have heard the slogan: "A little white lie never hurt anybody." But that couldn't be farther from the truth. Lying hurts your reputation and relationships with your friends and family, and it causes them not to trust you anymore. God always wants you to tell the truth no matter how difficult, painful, or awkward. He despises it when you lie to the people you love to cover up your mistakes. Just be honest, and your life will be much simpler.

Bedtime Prayer:

*Dear God, help me not to lie to anyone throughout my life.
Amen.*

DAY 123: WALK IN TRUTH

Scripture:
"Little children, let us not love in word or talk but in deed and in truth."

1 John 3:18 ESV

Explanation:
It can be hard to love everyone around you as a kid. But God doesn't just want you to walk and talk in love to those you know and don't know. He wants you to set an example of how to act in deed and truth. Telling the truth is one of the most important things to do. It will serve you well because people can trust and depend on you. So, walk in God's truth in word and deed every day.

Bedtime Prayer:
Dear God, please help me to love in deed and truth. Amen.

DAY 124: FEW WORDS

Scripture:
"Let what you say be simply 'Yes' or 'No'..."

Mathew 5:37 ESV

Explanation:
You learn to let your words be few very quickly because sometimes explaining yourself is a complete waste of time. A lot of people won't want to hear your side of stories. If you try to get your point across in school, with a bully, or with your family, let your words be few and let your actions show what a good Christian you are. Sometimes, the best thing to do is let your answers either be 'yes' or 'no' or remain silent, not saying anything.

Bedtime Prayer:
Dear God, please help my words be few. Amen.

DAY 125: WISDOM FROM ABOVE

Scripture:
"But the wisdom from above is first pure, then peaceable, gentle, open to reason..."

James 3:17 ESV

Explanation:
Wisdom from heaven comes when you ask God for guidance. It's pure, so you know, without a doubt, that it's God. Then God fills you with His everlasting peace and keeps your mind on track. Then, God asks you in your heart and mind whether or not you are ready to be open to reason. He does this either by name personally in your heart, or inaudibly in your mind. He already knows when you'll be ready to receive the things He will tell you.

Bedtime Prayer:

Dear God, please help me to be peaceful, gentle, and open to reason. Amen.

DAY 126: KEEP YOUR CONSCIENCE CLEAR

Scripture:
"So I always take pains to have a clear conscience toward both God and man."

Acts 24:16 ESV

Explanation:
As a Christian, you know the difference between right and wrong. Yes, you're not perfect and won't ever be perfect in any aspect, especially your interactions with people. You will mess up and say things you didn't mean to say. A clear conscience means apologizing when you know you're wrong and making appropriate changes. It also means never allowing people to bully you for your faith or apologize when you know you didn't do anything wrong. Ask Him for His guidance when trying to keep your conscience clear.

Bedtime Prayer:

Dear God, please help me to have a clear conscience toward you and others. Amen.

DAY 127: LOOK FORWARD

Scripture:
"Let your eyes look directly forward, and your gaze be straight before you."

Proverbs 4:25 ESV

Explanation:
Instead of looking back on your life and feeling depressed by your mistakes, look forward to the things you're yet to do. Instead of feeling guilty for the things you didn't accomplish, see every new day as an opportunity to learn and become a better person. God wants you to learn from your mistakes but doesn't want to punish you. Instead, look forward to His fantastic future ahead of you. Keep your eyes on the prize of going to heaven eventually.

Bedtime Prayer:

Dear God, help me to look forward instead of backward. Focus me on you. Amen.

DAY 128: BE HONEST

Scripture:
"Whoever gives an honest answer kisses the lips."

Proverbs 24:26 ESV

Explanation:
It will always make you feel better telling the truth than it will feel to lie to anyone in your life. When you lie, you feel uncomfortable, like walking on eggshells, hoping you don't crack under pressure to cover up one mistake after anoth-er. You wish that your secrets were never revealed. But God already knows when you lie. You can't hide anything from Him. Why wear yourself out by lying when you can have peace by telling the truth?

Bedtime Prayer:

Dear God, please help me always be honest and tell the truth. Amen.

DAY 129: FAITHFUL WITH A LOT

Scripture:
"One who is faithful in a very little is also faithful in much..."

Luke 16:10 ESV

Explanation:
Getting your allowance can be an exciting thing. You might want to buy something for yourself instead of putting your money in the bank for a rainy day. But God says whoever is faithful with a little will eventually be entrusted with a lot. That means that if you're smart with your allowance money now, you'll have more money in the future when you need it as an adult. God wants you to be careful and enjoy your money at the same time.

Bedtime Prayer:
Dear God, help me to be faithful with a little and a lot. Amen.

DAY 130: DON'T DECEIVE ANYONE

Scripture:
"Do not deceive with your lips."

Proverbs 24:28 ESV

Explanation:
Lying doesn't get you anywhere good in life. It only gets you more pain and uncertainty, and it causes your family and friends not to trust you anymore. Lying might seem easy at first, especially if it's "just a little white lie," but it's never the more straightforward path because people will discover the truth you're hiding from them. Eventually, God will already know you better than anyone. He sees and hears you whether you lie or tell the truth. Keep yourself from lying, and you'll feel better.

Bedtime Prayer:
*Dear God, help me not to deceive anyone with my words.
Amen.*

DAY 131: BE HUMBLE

Scripture:
"The reward for humility and fear of the Lord is riches and honor and life."

Proverbs 22:4 ESV

Explanation:
Being humble can be hard sometimes, especially if you just got on the basketball team at school or got a better grade on your math test than your brother. At those times and others, you will want to brag. But instead of telling others about your accomplishments, give God the honor, glory, and praise He deserves. Don't act like you're better than anyone. Thank God for what He helped you accomplish, and be humble. Don't seek attention.

Bedtime Prayer:
Dear God, please give me a long life that honors you. Amen.

DAY 132: HUMILITY

Scripture:
"For the Lord takes pleasure in his people; he adorns the humble with salvation."

Psalm 149:4 ESV

Explanation:
God doesn't like it when you brag. He'd rather you be humble and acknowledge that you didn't make it alone. He is the one who has helped you through every step of your life. He is the only reason you have made it this far. He takes pleasure in you when you give Him the acknowledgment for everything that you're able to accomplish. He smiles at you when you pass math, make a new friend, or own up to your parents for a mistake.

Bedtime Prayer:
Dear God, thank you for taking pleasure in me and saving me. Amen.

DAY 133: TEACHING YOU TO BE HUMBLE

Scripture:
"He leads the humble in what is right and teaches the humble his way."

Psalm 25:9 ESV

Explanation:
There will be times when it will be tough to resist bragging. If you get a new toy that your little sister wants more than you, a bigger weekly allowance or your grandma takes you out for lunch before your sibling, you might think you're better than them. But God wants you to be humble instead of bragging. Ask Him to teach you the right words to say and actions to take in front of your siblings.

Bedtime Prayer:

Dear Lor, teach me your ways. Amen.

DAY 134: GLORIFY GOD

Scripture:
"To our God and Father be glory forever and ever. Amen."

Philippians 4:20 ESV

Explanation:
Have you ever had an out-of-body experience when worshipping in church? It's incredible to experience God's wonder and majesty and to feel His presence firsthand during one of your favorite songs. It's OK to have tears streaming down your face and realizing how good God is to you. He saved you by dying on the cross for your sins and protects you from harm. He gives you peace in the middle of chaos because He loves you. To Him be the glory forever and ever.

Bedtime Prayer:

Dear God, help me to glorify you forever in heaven and on earth. Amen.

DAY 135: LEARN FROM GOD

Scripture
"What is man that you are mindful of him...?"

Psalm 8:4 ESV

Explanation:
Have you ever wondered, "Who am I that God loves me this much? What's so special about me?" Think about it. He made you in His image and has a beautiful, perfect plan for your life. God loves you so much that He is willing to do anything and everything to help you get and keep a personal relationship with you. He thinks you are worth dying for. Nothing will ever change His love for you, no matter how many mistakes you've made.

Bedtime Prayer:

Dear God, thank you for thinking so much of me. Amen.

DAY 136: LET OTHERS TALK YOU UP

Scripture:
Let another praise you, and not your own mouth; a stranger, and not your own lips."

Proverbs 27:2 ESV

Explanation:
When someone notices how well you did in school on your report card, let the teacher or your parents and grandparents acknowledge and congratulate you on the job well done. Let them say how proud of you they are. Don't brag about yourself with the "look at what I accomplished" attitude. Acknowledge their praise. Then, instead of praising yourself, praise God for helping you get good grades. Then, continue doing your best every day for the rest of the school year with God at your side.

Bedtime Prayer:

Dear God, help me not think highly of myself when others praise me. Amen.

DAY 137: STUMBLING

Scripture:
"For we all stumble in many ways..."

James 3:2 ESV

Explanation:
When you accidentally hurt your friend's feelings, you'll worry that you might lose them for good. When you get a bad grade on a test, detention, or an F on your report card, you'll worry about telling your parents because you know they'll be disappointed. Even in those situations, God doesn't look down on or think less of you. He already knew each mistake you'd make when He made you. He isn't mad at you for stumbling because each experience helps you learn and grow.

Bedtime Prayer:
Dear God, please help me remember that mistakes are okay. Amen.

DAY 138: BE ALERT AND REPENT

Scripture:
"Those whom I love, I reprove and discipline, so be zealous and repent."

Revelation 3:19 ESV

Explanation:
When you make a mistake and hurt someone with your words or actions, be the bigger person and apologize to them. Also, apologize to God for sinning against Him and ask Him for His forgiveness while repenting. Repenting means that you will spend the rest of your life doing your best to never sin in that same way again. God knows there will be times when you mess up; when you mess up, acknowledge it before God and ask Him to help you continue to learn from it.

Bedtime Prayer:
Dear God, Please help me to be alert and repent. Amen.

DAY 139: MY GRACE IS SUFFICIENT

Scripture:
"My grace is sufficient for you, for my power is made perfect in weakness."

2 Corinthians 12:9 ESV

Explanation:
When you feel like you can't go on, do you immediately turn to God or try to figure things out yourself? It can sometimes feel like you're the only one going through tough times in school, with friends, and at home. But God could be putting all those obstacles in your path to get your attention. Remember, His power is made perfect in your weakness. You can boast about your weaknesses because He has you covered.

Bedtime Prayer:
Dear God, thank you for your grace, which is always sufficient for me. Amen.

DAY 140: NO CONDEMNATION

Scripture:
"There is therefore now no condemnation for those who are in Christ Jesus."

Romans 8:1 ESV

Explanation:
Isn't it such a relief to know that no matter what you do wrong and no matter what choices you make in the future, you are saved, loved, and cherished by God? There is no condemnation for those who are in Christ Jesus. That means there is nothing you could do to change His love for you, and no way He would ever turn His back on you. Let your friends, family, and community know that once they're saved, they're also free of condemnation.

Bedtime Prayer:
Dear God, I praise you. I have no condemnation because I'm your child. Amen.

DAY 141: GOD'S WORD STANDS FOREVER

Scripture:
"The grass withers, the flower fades, but the word of our God will stand forever."

Isaiah 40:8 ESV

Explanation:
You might start getting discouraged about the constant changes in your life. You might move to a new neighborhood, change schools, make new friends, or change churches. The list of changes is endless. But there is one person who will stay the same forever. That's Jesus. Even though the seasons change yearly, the word of God and the promises He tells you in His Word will never change. He is the only person constantly the same in a world of change.

Bedtime Prayer:
Dear God, thank you that you will stand forever. You'll never fade away. Amen.

DAY 142: HIS UNDERSTANDING

Scripture:
"Great is our Lord, and abundant in power; his understanding is beyond measure."

Psalm 147:5 ESV

Explanation:
God's power is never-ending. His understanding is beyond your understanding. He literally knows everything about you. He knew you before you were born and knew precisely what you'd do in your life. He knows what is going to happen before you do. He knows how to handle every situation. He knows you better than you know yourself. He will give you the knowledge you need to get through life. Trust that He will guide you through each day and that He already has solutions to your problems.

Bedtime Prayer:
Dear God, please help me remember that your understanding is beyond mine. Amen.

DAY 143: I WILL MAKE A WAY

Scripture:
"Behold, I am doing a new thing; now it springs forth..."

Isaiah 43:18-19 ESV

Explanation:
You might get tired of doing things the same way. Doing math homework every evening can seem repetitive when you learn math during school. If you struggle when your parents fight, you'll wonder if God will or even can change the situation. Trust that He sees the mundane routines of homework and the stress of your parents fighting. He will make a way when there seems to be no way. When it feels like nothing's changing, it doesn't mean God isn't moving and working on your behalf.

Bedtime Prayer:

Dear God, please remind me that you will always make a way. Amen.

DAY 144: HOPE IS NOT CUT OFF

Scripture:
"Surely there is a future, and your hope will not be cut off."

Proverbs 23:18 ESV

Explanation:
Whenever your family member gets a diagnosis of cancer, you might feel like your whole world just collapsed. You will wonder if and how your family member will survive. But it's during those trying times that God wants you to know He is always with you. Your family's hope is not cut off. You will have a future with them, and they will get the proper treatment. You all will feel God's presence. Your family members will be made healthy and whole.

Bedtime Prayer:

Dear God, thank you for my future being secure in you. Amen.

DAY 145: GOD'S COUNSEL

Scripture:

"'My counsel shall stand, and I will accomplish all my purpose...'"

Isaiah 46:9-10 ESV

Explanation:

How often do you seek God's counsel and guidance throughout your day or week? It would be best to ask Him for advice about anything you're feeling and experiencing. Whether at school or home, you can always come before God and ask Him where to go and what to do. He is the only entirely trustworthy person. His counsel will stand forever, and He will help you accomplish the purpose He has set for you.

Bedtime Prayer:

Dear God, help me to seek you and believe I'll accomplish my purpose. Amen.

DAY 146: BODY OF CHRIST

Scripture:

"Now you are the body of Christ and individually members of it."

1 Corinthians 12:27 ESV

Explanation:

You might be wondering what it means to be the body of Christ. That means that you are the eyes, legs, hands, and feet of Jesus Himself. As soon as He became your Savior, it became your responsibility to share His love with others through your words and actions. You can share His hope, grace, compassion, and mercy with your friends, family, classmates, teachers, and coaches. Be the arms that reach out to people in need. Share His love with a smile. Don't judge people. Be His hands and feet.

Bedtime Prayer:

Dear God, thank you that I'm part of the body of Christ. Amen.

DAY 147: HE CHOSE YOU

Scripture:
"Even as he chose us in him before the foundation of the world..."

Ephesians 1:4 ESV

Explanation:
It can be hard to remember that God chose you as His child, especially during hard times. But He chose you because He loves you and has a great purpose for you in life. He chose you and knew His plan for you before He made the earth. How amazing is that! He wants you to walk the world and tell people how you were changed by His presence in your life. He chose you for specific assignments.

Bedtime Prayer:
Dear God, thank you for choosing me. Amen.

DAY 148: HE RAISED YOU UP

Scripture:
"And raised us up with him and seated us with him in the heavenly places in Christ Jesus."

Ephesians 2:6 ESV

Explanation:
Even though you haven't accomplished your true purpose on earth, do you believe you will be welcomed and raised up into heaven one day when your assignment on earth is done? You can be assured that you will be raised into eternal life and live with Jesus and God forever. There will be no more pain, second-guessing, or sorrow in heaven. But right now, He needs you on earth to fulfill your duties.

Bedtime Prayer:
Dear God, thank you for raising and seating me with Jesus in heaven. Amen.

DAY 149: FELLOW CITIZENS

Scripture:

So then you are no longer strangers and aliens, but you are fellow citizens."

Ephesians 2:19 ESV

Explanation:

You will most likely feel like an alien or an outsider when you move to a new school district and a new home. You might feel like an alien when you try to make new friends at school but get nowhere. You might feel like an alien at home if your parents don't spend quality time with you. Remember that you're God's daughter. You're never an alien to Him. He knows, loves, and calls you by name. You are a beloved citizen of heaven.

Bedtime Prayer:

Dear God, thank you for letting me know I belong to your kingdom. Amen.

DAY 150: BAPTIZED THROUGH CHRIST

Scripture:

"For as many of you as were baptized into Christ have put on Christ."

Galatians 3:27-28 ESV

Explanation:

When you were baptized, you were automatically given a very important assignment- to help others come to know Christ. How often do you show Christ's love and lead by His example? It doesn't matter where or how you talk about Him. It's ok on the playground, at home, or around your community. You can make significant differences in people's lives and tell them how a relationship with Jesus has changed yours for the best. Be an inspiration. Testify God's love through your words and actions.

Bedtime Prayer:

Dear God, thank you for saving me through baptism. Amen.

DAY 151: FRIENDS LOVE AT ALL TIMES

Scripture:
"A friend loves at all times, and a brother is born for adversity."

Proverbs 17:17 ESV

Explanation:
Love your friends no matter what they're going through. Let them know they can always trust in, confide in you, and count on you. Some girls you meet can become your best friends and people you consider sisters. The Bible says a friend always loves, and a brother (or sister) is born for adversity. Be the friend you want people to be for you. Be your friend's loyal sister in Christ. Never give up on your true friends.

Bedtime Prayer:
Dear God, help me be the friend who always loves others. Amen.

DAY 152: GODLY FRIENDSHIPS

Scripture:
"A man of many companions may come to ruin..."

Proverbs 18:24 ESV

Explanation:
Godly friendships are more important than having many friends who negatively influence your life and harm your faith. It's better to have a few close friends that lead you closer to God than many selfish, so-called friends pushing you away from Him. Ask God who you should and shouldn't be friends with, and see where He leads you. See who He leads you to be friends with at school, church, and community.

Bedtime Prayer:
Dear God, help me to make a few genuine Godly friends. Amen.

DAY 153: IRON SHARPENS IRON

Scripture:
"Iron sharpens iron, and one man sharpens another."

Proverbs 27:17 ESV

Explanation:
You probably know how it feels to sit alone at the school lunch table while praying you make friends. When God gave you that friend, you were forever thankful. You both look out for and encourage each other. That's what it means when God says iron sharpens iron. Whenever you offer encouraging words to your friends or family, you're being the person God created you to be. God uses you to sharpen people's belief in Jesus and to help them believe in themselves, too.

Bedtime Prayer:

Dear God, help me to strengthen my friends with your encouragement. Amen.

DAY 154: BE A SWEET FRIEND

Scripture:
"...the sweetness of a friend comes from his earnest counsel."

Proverbs 27:9 ESV

Explanation:
Not having a friend be there for you when you need them the most is complicated. If you don't get emotional support from your friends, you can still support them emotionally. Hopefully, they will start doing the same for you. Be there for them in the same way that God is there for you. Hug them instead of offering advice. If they ask for advice, be gentle in response to their problem. Be the sweet friend that you want others to be for you.

Bedtime Prayer:

Dear God, help me speak sweetly to my friends and give them your advice. Amen.

DAY 155: TWO ARE BETTER THAN ONE

Scripture:
"Two are better than one, because they have a good reward for their toil..."

Ecclesiastes 4:9-10 ESV

Explanation:
Have you ever noticed that it is harder to get school projects done when you don't have a partner? Handling school projects alone can be overwhelming. Having someone help you takes some of the weight off of you. The two of you working together makes the project easier and faster. It enables you to learn to work together and share your unique vision and ideas. It's better to work together than alone because you'll get a reward for your hard work from your teacher and God.

Bedtime Prayer:

Dear God, help us to work together on school projects. Amen.

DAY 156: DON'T WITHHOLD KINDNESS

Scripture:
"He who withholds kindness from a friend forsakes the fear of the Almighty."

Job 6:14 ESV

Explanation:
Some days, you will be in a bad mood and want to argue with your friends over dumb things like who has the better hairstyle or whose mom packed the better lunch. You'd rather be mean instead of being kind. You shouldn't be mean to your friends just because you're struggling. Jesus is your most faithful friend. He is always kind to you. So, do your best to be kind to your friends. Jesus is proud of you when you're kind to your friends instead of mean.

Bedtime Prayer:

Dear God, teach me never to withhold kindness because you've never withheld kindness from me. Amen.

DAY 157: DON'T BEFRIEND ANGRY PEOPLE

Scripture:
"Make no friendship with a man given to anger..."

Proverbs 22:24 ESV

Explanation:
If you've ever seen your father, mother, or extended family member explode for no reason multiple times, that could mean they're prone to anger. The Bible warns you to stay away from anyone who gets angry quickly. God even says not to make friends with anyone prone to becoming angry. God is trying to protect you from mental and emotional pain. He's telling you how you can avoid it by staying away from angry people. Ask Him to protect you and your peace of mind.

Bedtime Prayer:

Dear God, please help me never to be friends with someone who is angry all the time. Amen

DAY 158: FAITHFUL WORDS

Scripture:
"Faithful are the wounds of a friend; profuse are the kisses of an enemy."

Proverbs 27:6 ESV

Explanation:
It's better to make friends with a few people who are faithful and devoted to God than to have many people talking wrong about you behind your back. It's better to have people stand up for you and protect you when you're not around. Be the faithful friend people can trust. Tell the truth even if it hurts. It's better to be honest and hurt a friend versus telling them things they'd rather hear. Remember, if you lie, you could destroy the friendship forever.

Bedtime Prayer:
Dear God, please help me to use excellent and faithful judgments with friends. Amen.

DAY 159: WALK WITH THE WISE, NOT WITH FOOLS

Scripture:
"Whoever walks with the wise becomes wise, but the companion of fools will suffer harm."

Proverbs 13:20 ESV

Explanation:
If you've ever gotten the feeling in your gut that something is wrong, trust it. That's God speaking to you. Start walking with wise people in your friends and family circle at a young age. God says whoever walks with the wise will be wise, but those who walk with fools will get hurt. Speak up and say, "I don't want to do this." If you get mocked, then those people aren't your friends. Wouldn't you instead learn how to be wise now and in the future?

Bedtime Prayer:

Dear God, please help me find who is wise and foolish to hang out with. Amen.

DAY 160: DON'T SPREAD GOSSIP

Scripture:
"A whisperer separates close friends."

Proverbs 16:28 ESV

Explanation:
It's important not to engage in gossip, even though it can seem like fun. In the long run, talking badly about someone behind their back can cost someone their reputation. Gossip can also cause you to develop trust issues with people. People won't trust you with their secrets because they know you'll tell someone else. A whisper separates close friends. Stand firm in your beliefs if your so-called friends mock you for not engaging in gossip. Stay away from gossip so you don't lose the precious friends that God gave you.

Bedtime Prayer:

Dear God, please help me not gossip. Amen.

DAY 161: DON'T ABANDON YOUR FRIENDS

Scripture:
"Do not forsake your friend..."

Proverbs 27:10 ESV

Explanation:
If you've ever had a good friend walk out of your life for no reason, you know how painful it is. You automatically start wondering what you did wrong and blaming yourself for what you could have done better to keep the friendship. You might never know what happened between you both. But don't walk away from them altogether. You can still pray for them and wish them the best without inviting them into your life again. Don't forsake them because God has never forsaken you.

Bedtime Prayer:

Dear God, please help me never abandon my friends when they need me. Amen.

DAY 162: WISDOM FOR YOUR FUTURE

Scripture:
"Listen to advice and accept instruction, that you may gain wisdom in the future."

Proverbs 19:20 ESV

Explanation:
How many times per day in school do you have that thought of "yeah, yeah. I already learned this"? All kids feel bored in school and in life when their teachers and parents teach them something that they think they already know well. But God wants you to listen to all the advice they give you. Pay close attention to what your parents give you. Whatever they're teaching you might seem repetitive and boring right now. But they're teaching you different things you need to know for your future.

Bedtime Prayer:

Dear God, teach me to gain your wisdom for my future. Amen.

DAY 163: ENCOURAGE PEOPLE TO DO GOOD WORK

Scripture:
"And let us consider how to stir up one another to love and good works."

Hebrews 10:24-25 ESV

Explanation:
If your church has ever had the opportunity to help serve others in your city, did you and your family and friends jump at the chance to change people's lives? Your younger siblings may not want to participate because they think it's boring. You can talk to them and show them how much fun it is to serve God's people in different ways. Stir up their excitement by making the service project a game you play together as the one who collects the most leaves wins.

Bedtime Prayer:

Dear God, please help me to encourage people to do your good works. Amen.

DAY 164: WHEN FRIENDS BETRAY YOU

Scripture:
"My friends scorn me; my eye pours out tears to God..."

Job 16:20 ESV

Explanation:
Job is one of the most Godly yet sad people in the Bible and worldwide. God put him through so much, but Job didn't stop praising God through every hardship. Even when his true friends had abandoned him for staying true to his faith, he knew staying strong in his faith was his only choice. When your friends betray you in ways you never expected to be hurt, rest assured that God will never betray or leave you questioning His love for you.

Bedtime Prayer:

Dear God, when friends turn their backs on me, keep me strong. Amen

DAY 165: BEAR EACH OTHER'S BURDENS

Scripture:
"Bear one another's burdens, and so fulfill the law of Christ."

Galatians 6:2 ESV

Explanation:
You might wonder, " Why in the world would I want to take what my friends are going through and put it on my shoulders?" The answer is simple. It's because Jesus took all of your burdens and the burdens of every person in the world upon Himself on the cross and sacrificed Himself for all of us. He sacrificed the ultimate burden of dying for you in your place. Bear one another's burdens so that you fulfill the love of Christ through your words and actions.

Bedtime Prayer:

Dear God, please help me to bear my friends' burdens and support them. Amen.

DAY 166: MUTUAL ENCOURAGEMENT

Scripture:
"That is, that we may be mutually encouraged by each other's faith, both yours and mine."

Romans 1:12 ESV

Explanation:
It is important to get encouragement weekly from people. When people encourage you, it keeps your hope alive. Promoting your siblings, parents, friends, teachers, classmates, and coaches is also important. You truly never know what people are going through. They could be fighting private battles that they don't tell others about. Be an encouragement whenever you see anybody who looks sad, upset, angry, or depressed. Tell them that God loves them, is there for them, and that they will come through their struggles stronger than before.

Bedtime Prayer:

Dear God, help my friends and I encourage each other with our faith. Amen.

DAY 167: LONG TO SEE FRIENDS

Scripture:
"For I long to see you, that I may impart to you some spiritual gift to strengthen you..."

Romans 1:11 ESV

Explanation:
When you haven't seen your best friends for a while, you really miss them. You long to see them and spend time with them. When you're with them, you catch up about everything from school, sports, family, and pets. You might bring up how your faith has changed your life. If one of your friends doesn't know Jesus, you can pray for and with them. Be brave enough to share your spiritual gifts with your friends and help them know Jesus as their Savior.

Bedtime Prayer:
Dear God, please help me to share my spiritual gifts with my friends and family. Amen.

DAY 168: GATHER IN MY NAME

Scripture:
"For where two or three are gathered in my name, there am I among them."

Mathew 18:20 ESV

Explanation:
Whenever you encounter difficulties, don't you want a comforting hug from your friend or family member? Do you think about praying when an obstacle is in your path? When you pray, God hears every word you say in the stillness of your heart or out loud. Pray with others, too. Remember, whenever you, your family, or friends pray together, He is there among you. So, gather as many family members and friends as possible and have a prayer warrior session. He will continually make a difference in people's lives.

Bedtime Prayer:
Dear God, thank you for being with me and my family when we pray. Amen

DAY 169: BUILD OTHERS UP

Scripture:
"Let no corrupting talk come out of your mouths, but only such as is good for building up..."

Ephesians 4:29 ESV

Explanation:
As a kid, you probably let unwholesome talk and bad words come out of your mouth. You've probably told your siblings to shut up and go away and got yelled at by your parents. But it's important to remember that God doesn't want you to be mean or hurtful with your words. He doesn't want any mean or hateful words from your mouth. Think before you speak. Only build people up with your words. Don't tear people down.

Bedtime Prayer:
Dear God, keep any filthy talk out of my mouth. Amen.

DAY 170: DON'T MAKE FRIENDS WITH BLABBERS

Scripture:
"Whoever goes about slandering reveals secrets; therefore do not associate with a simple babbler."

Proverbs 20:19 ESV

Explanation:
As fun as it can be to listen to and hear gossip, don't engage in it. If you gossip, you will be tempted to repeat what you hear to other people. If one of your friends comes to you and tells you a deep secret about their life in confidence, that means that they don't want you to tell anyone else about it. If you tell their secret, you break their trust. The Bible tells you not to associate with a simple babbler, so don't start being one.

Bedtime Prayer:
Dear God, help me not reveal anything that's said to me in confidence. Amen.

DAY 171: GRATITUDE

Scripture:
"Give thanks in all circumstances; for this is the will of God in Christ Jesus for you."

1 Thessalonians 5:18 ESV

Explanation:
"How do I give thanks in every situation, even when I feel sad or angry?" You aren't the only one who has asked that question. God wants you to try your best to be grateful in any and every situation because knowing how to control your feelings and emotions will help you throughout your life. It is also God's will for you to be thankful in all circumstances. No matter what you're going through, you can be grateful for everything you have.

Bedtime Prayer:
Dear God, please help me to be grateful and give thanks in all circumstances. Amen

DAY 172: THE DAY THE LORD HAS MADE

Scripture:
"This is the day that the Lord has made; let us rejoice and be glad in it."

Psalm 118:24 ESV

Explanation:
Every day you spend with the people you love is an incredible gift. You never know what could happen any day, so enjoy every minute. Every day, instead of waking up on the wrong side of the bed, change your attitude. Don't let anything steal your joy. Be grateful that God gave you another day of life. He has beautiful plans for you, and each day, He helps you fulfill them. No matter what, there is always something to be thankful for.

Bedtime Prayer:
Dear God, please let me rejoice every day instead of being grumpy. Amen

DAY 173: A PART OF HIS KINGDOM

Scripture:
"Therefore let us be grateful for receiving a kingdom that cannot be shaken..."

Hebrews 12:28 ESV

Explanation:
Did you know that as soon as you accepted Jesus as your Lord and Savior, you were automatically accepted into His heavenly kingdom? You might wonder, "How can I be accepted into heaven when I'm still on earth?" Jesus died for you on the cross and received you as part of His Kingdom. His holy kingdom can't ever be shaken. Nothing will ever take you of God's kingdom. Wouldn't you rather be a part of the heavenly kingdom of God than part of the kingdom of the world?

Bedtime Prayer:

Dear God, thank you for accepting me into your kingdom, which can't be shaken. Amen.

DAY 174: GOD'S PEACE IN YOUR HEART

Scripture:
"And let the peace of Christ rule in your hearts..."

Colossians 3:15 ESV

Explanation:
Keeping God's everlasting peace in your heart can sometimes be tricky. Those are tricky things to get through when you're struggling with school, making friends, or didn't make the sports team. Despite those challenges, you can turn to God anytime and ask Him to help you. You can cling to God's everlasting peace. His peace surpasses all understanding. Let it fill your heart, mind, and soul. He will carry you through every obstacle. Rest in His peace today.

Bedtime Prayer:

Dear God, please put your everlasting peace in my heart and soul. Amen.

DAY 175: SING HIS PRAISES

Scripture:

"...Come into his presence with singing!...

Psalm 100:1-5 ESV

Explanation:

"Can I go into God's presence at any time? Am I really in God's sight at all times?" Those questions might pop into your head from time to time. No matter where you are- whether you're walking to school, riding the bus, riding your bike, studying for a test, or playing kickball with your friends, you can praise God at any time, no matter what you're do- ing. Take every opportunity to honor God with singing. Even if you don't have a good singing voice, praise Him anyway.

Bedtime Prayer:

Dear God, please help me sing my heart out to you daily.
Amen.

DAY 176: GRATEFUL IN EVERY WAY

Scripture:

"In every way and everywhere we accept this with all grati-
tude."

Acts 24:3 ESV

Explanation:

God sent His only Son, Jesus, to die for you on the cross. Learning to praise and thank Him for saving your life is im- portant from a young age. The more you know about Him, the more you'll want to praise Him for what He's done. Each new day, the beauty of the world around you- the ocean, mountains, deserts, and sunset colors. You can always look to heaven and thank Him for His goodness.

Bedtime Prayer:

Dear God, help me to accept what you've done in every way
gratefully. Amen.

DAY 177: GOD'S GRACE IS NOT IN VAIN

Scripture:
"But by the grace of God I am what I am, and his grace to-ward me was not in vain."

1 Corinthians 15:10 ESV

Explanation:
"No one likes me. No one wants to be my friend. I'm not pretty, popular, or smart enough." All girls have those nasty thoughts about themselves while looking at themselves in the mirror. Don't let those negative thoughts win. God doesn't think you're ugly at all. He will let you get on the correct sports team and make the right friends at the right time. He sees you as His precious daughter. By His grace, you are who you are. Rest assured, His grace toward you isn't in vain.

Bedtime Prayer:

Dear God, thank you for your grace towards me, which is never in vain. Amen.

DAY 178: YOUR STRENGTH AND YOUR SHEILD

Scripture:
"The Lord is my strength and my shield; in him my heart trusts, and I am helped;"

Psalm 28:7 ESV

Explanation:
When going through tough battles such as bullying, struggling in sports, or not understanding science, math, or history, God wants you to remember that He is there for you at all times. He wants to be your strength when you feel like your strength is running out. He wants to be your shield and protect you from the negativity in the world. Allow Him to be the strength and shield of your life. Trust Him that things will work out. Declare that Jesus is your strength and shield.

Bedtime Prayer:

Dear God, please remind me that you're my strength and shield. Amen.

DAY 179 GOD'S CHOSEN DAUGHTER

Scripture:
"Put on then, as God's chosen ones, holy and beloved, compassionate hearts, kindness, humility...."

Colossians 3:12 ESV

Explanation:
No matter how negative you feel about yourself, God wants you to realize the truth. You were made in His image. You are His holy, precious daughter. He wants your heart to be full of kindness, beloved compassion, and humility, not just toward yourself but also towards everyone else around you. He wants you to think kindly about yourself and the way you interact with others in your life. When you are compassionate towards yourself, you'll be compassionate towards others.

Bedtime Prayer:

Dear God, thank you that I'm one of your chosen people. Amen.

DAY 180: REJOICE AND SUFFER WITH ONE ANOTHER

Scripture:
"If one member suffers, all suffer together; if one member is honored, all rejoice together."

1 Corinthians 12:26 ESV

Explanation:
Have you ever seen people in church be sad when someone mentions a death in their family, and then they rejoice whenever a child gets baptized or accepts Jesus as their Savior? They do that because God commands everyone to rejoice with those who rejoice and be happy for them. He wants you to join people in their time of celebration, too. He also wants you to mourn with anyone who mourns. Be the friend God wants you to be, whether someone is grieving or rejoicing.

Bedtime Prayer:

Dear God, teach me to rejoice or mourn with anyone as you do. Amen.

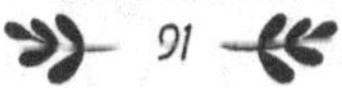

DAY 181: JESUS WEEPS FOR YOU

Scripture:
"Jesus wept."

John 11:35 ESV

Explanation:
Sometimes, it can feel like Jesus doesn't care about you.
But that couldn't be farther from the truth. Jesus physically
wept when He found out that His close friend Lazarus had
died. He weeps for you when you're sad, angry, and upset.
It doesn't matter how young you are. God loves you and
mourns with you. Jesus intercedes on your behalf, asking
God to take your pain away. He never likes seeing you upset,
scared, or doubting yourself. He feels all the emotions you
feel.

Bedtime Prayer:

*Dear God, thank you for weeping with me just like you did
with Lazarus. Amen.*

DAY 182: GOD SYMPATHIZES WITH YOU

Scripture:
*"...we do not have a high priest who is unable to sympathize
with our weaknesses..."*

Hebrews 4:15 ESV

Explanation:
Isn't it amazing to know you have a heavenly Father who
sympathizes with you whenever you struggle? He is never
immune to your pain just because He is in heaven. That's
why He sent His one and only Son, Jesus, to earth to take
away all the pain and sin everyone was living in. He never
stops loving you. He never stops interceding on your behalf.
He asks His heavenly Father to stop the pain you're dealing
with, no matter how big or small the pain might be.

Bedtime Prayer:

*Dear God, thank you for always sympathizing with me when
I'm sad. Amen.*

DAY 183: JESUS WAS TEMPTED TOO

Scripture:
"...but one who in every respect has been tempted as we are, yet without sin."

Hebrews 4:15 ESV

Explanation:
You might find it hard to believe that Jesus was tempted in His earthly life. But it's true. He was tempted to jump off a building, worship someone other than God, and ask if He could turn stones into bread. He was starving when He was tempted. But He never gave into any of the temptations. So the next time you're hungry and want to give into temptation, remember how Jesus stood firm in His unwavering faith. If Jesus could do it, so can you.

Bedtime Prayer:

Dear God, thank you that you were tempted just like I am. Amen.

DAY 184: PURE IN HEART

Scripture:
"Blessed are the pure in heart, for they shall see God."

Matthew 5:8 ESV

Explanation:
Have you ever heard the term "pure in heart?" That means putting God before everything else in your life and making Him your top priority, no matter how old you are. Being pure in heart can also mean that you recognize that you're a sinner. You know you need God's forgiveness and ask Him for it daily. You're blessed because you can see God as your heavenly Father, Jesus as your Savior, and the Holy Spirit as your helper in making decisions about your faith.

Bedtime Prayer:

Dear God, thank you for the blessing of knowing you and being pure in heart. Amen.

DAY 185: CLEAN HEART AND RIGHT SPIRIT

Scripture:

"Create in me a clean heart, O God, and renew a right spirit within me."

Psalm 51:10 ESV

Explanation:

When you sin, do you always automatically ask God for forgiveness? You might ask, "But how do I ask Him to forgive, lead, and guide me in His ways?" Come before Him and admit that you're a sinner and need His help. You can't get a clean heart on your own. Ask God to renew your body, heart, mind, and soul. Don't be afraid to ask Him to clean out your heart. Ask Him to lead you in His ways and to make you a better person.

Bedtime Prayer:

Dear God, please create a clean heart and right spirit within me. Amen.

DAY 186: GOD GIVES YOU LIFE

Scripture:

"Turn my eyes from looking at worthless things; and give me life in your ways."

Psalm 119:37 ESV

Explanation:

Did you watch a movie or a TV show unsuitable for children your age, and your parents didn't want you to watch it? Have you talked badly about yourself lately? If you've done any or more of these things, you're only hurting yourself. God wants you to live your life worshipping Him in your thoughts, words, and actions. It means watching what you put before your eyes. Honor Him in the things you listen to. Ask Him to help you focus on heavenly things, not earthly things.

Bedtime Prayer:

Dear God, keep me from looking at worthless things. Give me life in your ways. Amen

DAY 187: CRUCIFIED WITH CHRIST

Scripture:
"I have been crucified with Christ..."

Galatians 2:20 ESV

Explanation:
"What does it mean to be crucified with Christ?" you might be asking. God sent His one and only Son, Jesus, to die on the cross for the forgiveness of your sins. He thought of you as He was hanging on the cross. He took away all of your sins because He loves you. All of your sins were cast away as far as the East is from the West. He took them all, so you no longer have to feel ashamed of what you've said and done wrong.

Bedtime Prayer:

Dear God, thank you for saving me through your death on the cross. Amen

DAY 188: FOCUS ON THINGS IN HEAVEN

Scripture:
"Set your minds on things that are above, not on things that are on earth."

Colossians 3:2 ESV

Explanation:
Whenever things go wrong, think about the positive things instead of thinking negatively. Think about the things that you'll get to experience in heaven. You'll be walking along streets that are paved with gold. You'll see the beauty and majesty of God's glory. You have peace and get to worship God forever. Think about seeing your family and friends that went to heaven ahead of you. You'll know everyone there too. Heaven is your forever home, while Earth is only your temporary home.

Bedtime Prayer:

Dear God, help me to focus on heavenly things instead of earthly things. Amen.

DAY 189: EVERY WORD FROM GOD IS TRUE

Scripture:
"Every word of God proves true; he is a shield to those who take refuge in him."

Proverbs 30:5 ESV

Explanation:
If you've ever wondered if God's words were true, they all are true. He keeps His promises and wants to prove His everlasting love to you. He is your everlasting peace and shield in times of trouble, darkness, and shame. He has shielded you from everything, including not passing tests or classes in school, car accidents, natural disasters, and losing friends and family members from illness. Every word Jesus said is true. He wants to continue protecting you and prove His words are true.

Bedtime Prayer:
Dear God, please help me believe your word is true. Amen.

DAY 190: FULL ASSURANCE OF FAITH

Scripture:
"Let us draw near with a true heart in full assurance of faith..."

Hebrews 22:10 ESV

Explanation:
Having the full assurance of your faith can be challenging with all of the distractions in your life. People, places, and things will distract you from keeping God at the forefront of your life. School, home life, and hanging with friends should draw you closer to God instead of pushing you away. Keeping your faith strong takes work, patience, and perseverance. God will give you the reassurance you need in His timing and His ways. You'll be able to have peace amongst chaos and praise Him no matter what.

Bedtime Prayer:
Dear God, please help me draw near you and be assured of my faith. Amen.

DAY 191: KEEP GOD'S TESTIMONIES

Scripture:

"Blessed are those who keep his testimonies, who seek him with their whole heart..."

Psalm 119:2 ESV

Explanation:

God's testimonies are the ones you hear from your friends and family when they tell you what great things God is doing in their lives. Reading your Bible teaches you the amazing things He has done for His people. You're one of God's chosen people. So, tell others about it whenever He does fantastic things in your life. Proclaim your testimonies of His goodness, grace, and mercy. Seek Him with all your heart daily. Who knows whose life you could be impacting? Share your testimony whenever possible.

Bedtime Prayer:

Dear God, please help me keep your testimonies in my heart daily. Amen.

DAY 192: PURE WORDS

Scripture:

"The words of the Lord are pure words..."

Psalm 112:6 ESV

Explanation:

You can learn to speak pure words throughout your life. Pure words are words that uplift, show kindness, and encourage people. The words you speak from your heart encourage people to praise God no matter what they're going through. God's pure words bring sweetness and peace to people's lives. God made Jesus the only pure and blameless one on earth. Everything He said was pure because He was both a true God and a true man. Let Jesus' words spill into your heart like a refreshing cold glass of water.

Bedtime Prayer:

Dear God, help me speak your pure words to everyone I meet. Amen

DAY 193: YOU'RE GOD'S CHILD

Scripture:
"Beloved, we are God's children now..."

1 John 3:2-3 ESV

Explanation:
Many children have been adopted by loving families. Maybe you're one of them. To be adopted means that you're loved and accepted unconditionally by your new family. You were automatically adopted and welcomed into God's family when you got baptized. You're not just your parent's daughter. You're also God's precious daughter whom He has chosen to do great things. Being adopted can be one of the greatest blessings in your life. But the ultimate blessing is being adopted into God's family through salvation in Jesus Christ.

Bedtime Prayer:

Dear God, thank you for adopting me as your child. Amen

DAY 194: SECRET PLACES IN YOUR HEART

Scripture:
"you teach me wisdom in the secret heart."

Psalm 51:6 ESV

Explanation:
Who knows you better than anyone else? You might be thinking of your friends and family members, such as your parents, siblings, grandparents, aunts, uncles, cousins, and maybe even your pets. But the person who knows you better than anyone else is Jesus. He knows the secret places in your heart where you keep all joy, sadness, and every other emotion. He is always ready, willing, and able to teach you how to gain wisdom about His love, grace, and mercy. Keep it safe in the secret of your heart.

Bedtime Prayer:

Dear God, teach me to be wise in the secret place of my heart. Amen.

DAY 195: MAY YOUR LOVE ABOUND

Scripture:
"And it is my prayer that your love may abound more and more...."

Philippians 1:9-10 ESV

Explanation:
How often do you tell the people that you love them? One a day, multiple times a day, once a week? Always tell people you love them. You can tell people you love them through your words and your actions. Hug your mom and dad before you go to school. Help your younger siblings if they struggle in sports or with their homework. Take a hot meal for your elderly neighbor, and call your grandparents. Jesus even prays that your love for people abounds (increases) more and more.

Bedtime Prayer:

Dear God, please help my love for you and others grow daily. Amen.

DAY 196: TAKE EVERY THOUGHT CAPTIVE

Scripture:
"...take every thought captive to obey Christ..."

2 Corinthians 10:5 ESV

Explanation:
You may not think how much your thoughts can positively and negatively affect you. For example, if you hear that a family member is sick, you might automatically start feeling anxious. If you get a bad grade on a test, you might feel angry with yourself. God doesn't want you to feel nervous, unhappy, or angry at yourself. He wants you to take your thoughts captive and think good thoughts. Change your negativity to positivity so your mind obeys Christ. He makes ways when there seems to be no way.

Bedtime Prayer:

Dear God, please help me keep my thoughts captivated by you. Amen.

DAY 197: GRACIOUS WORDS

Scripture:
"...gracious words are pure."

Proverbs 15:26 ESV

Explanation:
Gracious words are pure, especially when they come from God. When He puts someone on your mind and tells you to pray for them, He can fill your mind with the right words. God's words are pure and gracious to you, too. He speaks to you in the stillness of your heart and tells you what to do and where to go. You can spread His gracious words to everyone, including your teachers, family, coaches, and friends. Share your supply of gracious words from God today.

Bedtime Prayer:

Dear God, please help my words to be gracious and pure.
Amen.

DAY 198: JOY OF THE LORD

Scripture:
"...for the joy of the Lord is your strength."

Nehemiah 8:10 ESV

Explanation:
Whenever you feel you can't go on, do you pick yourself up and continue? God supplied you with His never-ending strength, resilience, and perseverance. Do you ever feel that unexplainable lift in your spirit among suffering? God fills you with joy. He fills you with joy when you think your life is crumbling. He gives you peace amongst the chaos and calmness in any storm of life. Don't let the storms of life steal the joy that God is willing, ready, and able to give you.

Bedtime Prayer:

Dear God, please put your joy and strength in my life again.
Amen.

DAY 199: GOD GIVES YOU REST

Scripture:
"Come to me, all who labor and are heavy laden, and I will give you rest."

Mathew 28:11 ESV

Explanation:
Where do you go when you need a rest for your mind, body, and soul? Go to God whenever you feel burdened. He will give you rest for your soul and put your mind at ease as soon as you start praying. He will take away your physical, emotional, and mental pain. He doesn't want you to feel ashamed to come to Him or think you're too broken to ask Him for His help. He is ready, willing, and able to help you at a moment's notice.

Bedtime Prayer:
Dear God, please give my body, mind, and soul rest in your arms. Amen.

DAY 200: EQUIPPED WITH GOD'S STRENGTH

Scripture:
"The God who equipped me with strength and made my way blameless."

Psalm 18:32 ESV

Explanation:
God equips you with the strength you need daily. He gives you His strength to push yourself beyond your physical limits in your sports games and helps you reach beyond your mental limits when you finally understand math. You feel free for the first time when you realize your strength wears out, but God's strength never weakens or goes away. Lean on Him for His never-ending strength. Don't ever be ashamed of yourself when you know you need His guidance. In God's eyes, you're blameless and perfect.

Bedtime Prayer:
Dear God, please help me and equip me with your strength. Amen.

DAY 201: THE END

Scripture:
"Better is the end of a thing than its beginning..."

Ecclesiastes 7:8 ESV

Explanation:
Sometimes, the end of a friendship is better than the beginning of it. Ask God to reveal the person's true character if someone hurts you and claims to be your friend. Sometimes, God lets things that are important to you come to an end so that you know who is truly there for you. Remember, no matter how bad it feels to lose a friend, God will replace them with an even better friend. The end is much better than your beginning because you will be in heaven forever.

Bedtime Prayer:
Dear God, remind me that the end is only the beginning in you. Amen

DAY 202: ONE DAY OR 1,000 YEARS

Scripture:
"...with the Lord one day is as a thousand years, and a thousand years as one day."

2 Peter 3:8 ESV

Explanation:
It is excellent to know that in God's eyes, one day is one thousand years, and one thousand years is only one day. That means God doesn't need time to stop Him from what He can and will do in your life. Nothing will ever stop God from fulfilling His plan for your life. Time doesn't stop for God or you. God takes time into His own hands. Whatever you think might take forever, God can make it go by quickly. Thank God for the bad times that He allows to pass quickly.

Bedtime Prayer:
Dear God, thank you for making 1,000 years one day in your eyes. Amen

DAY 203: GOD IS MERCIFUL AND GRACIOUS

Scripture:
"The Lord is merciful and gracious, slow to anger and abounding in steadfast love."

Psalm 103:8 ESV

Explanation:
God is, always has been, and always will be merciful and gracious, and slow to anger. He abounds in love for you every day. No matter what happens, His love for you will never change. He extends His mercy and forgiveness when He forgives you for your wrongdoings. Do your best to never take advantage of how good God is. Don't continue sinning. Ask God to help change how your heart feels and make you more merciful, gracious, and abounding in love towards the people in your life.

Bedtime Prayer:
Dear God, thank you for abounding in love for me. Amen.

DAY 204: FAVOR FOR A LIFETIME

Scripture:
"For his anger is but for a moment, and his favor is for a life-time..."

Psalm 30:5 ESV

Explanation:
Remember how much God loves you whenever you doubt yourself. His favor over your life has extended from when He first thought of you until you join Him in heaven. He will continue to favor your life until you go to heaven. To know that God has His lifetime favor upon you should make you stop worrying about what others think of you. You only need to concentrate on what God thinks of you, what He tells you to do, and where He leads you.

Bedtime Prayer:
Dear God, thank you that your favor on me lasts a lifetime. Amen.

DAY 205: JOY COMES IN THE MORNING

Scripture:
"Weeping may tarry for the night, but joy comes with the morning."

Psalm 30:5 ESV

Explanation:
If you ever feel sad or depressed, remember that while your feelings may last for the night, God's mercies are new every morning. Weeping may last the night, but His joy will always come in the morning. Ask Him to remove your sadness and remind you how much He loves you. He has gotten you through difficult times. He can and will do it again. Whenever you're sad, ask Him to remind you that no amount of sadness lasts forever. He will help you feel excited about your future.

Bedtime Prayer:
Dear God, thank you for your joy, which is new every morning. Amen.

DAY 206: ENDURE TILL THE END

Scripture:
"But the one who endures to the end will be saved."

Mathew 24:13 ESV

Explanation:
Never give up on your faith. Keep it strong by praying, reading God's word, and attending church every week. Staying close to God in a world of distractions is very important. Everything from school, sports, homework, and family can distract you from spending time with God. As you wake up, whisper thanks for another day of life. Ask Him to guide you through each obstacle if your day gets complicated. God will help you endure each day of your life with joy until the end when He calls you home.

Bedtime Prayer:
Dear God, thank you for helping me endure life until I see you in heaven. Amen.

DAY 207: PATIENT ENDURANCE

Scripture:
"And thus Abraham, having patiently waited, obtained the promise."

Hebrews 6:15 ESV

Explanation:
Waiting for your birthday or Christmas morning to come so you can open your gifts can be tiring. It can seem like the day will never come, but God is teaching you how important it is to wait patiently. Abraham had to wait many years to have a child and waited patiently for God to give him the gift of a son. Eventually, Abraham obtained his promise from God. The same thing will happen for you. If you wait patiently, you will also receive the promise of eternal life.

Bedtime Prayer:

Dear God, help me to wait patiently for you, just like Abraham. Amen.

DAY 208: HOPE OF THE RIGHTEOUS

Scripture:
"The hope of the righteous brings joy."

Proverbs 10:28 ESV

Explanation:
Do you want to be a vessel of hope among your friends and family, but you aren't sure how? Ask God to help you know how to be a vessel of hope to them. You can be a vessel of hope through your kind words to your parents, grandparents, teachers, siblings, and coaches. Through your actions, you can pray for and with people who want to know more about the hope Jesus brought to your life. Take every opportunity to be a vessel of hope for the Lord.

Bedtime Prayer:

Dear God, keep me from losing my hope. Keep me strong. Amen.

DAY 209: DIRECT YOUR HEARTS TO GOD

Scripture:
"May the Lord direct your hearts to the love of God and to the steadfastness of Christ."

2 Thessalonians 3:5 ESV

Explanation:
If you ever feel lost, never be afraid to go directly to God and ask Him to help bring your focus back towards Him and everything He has done for you. Say a prayer of thanks for each new day. Read His word to learn about Him. Direct your heart to His love and steadfastness. You can even bring others to know and love Christ by telling them how He saved your life. Do your best to keep your focus on Him at all times.

Bedtime Prayer:

Dear God, please help me to keep my heart focused on you. Amen.

DAY 210: GOD TAKES YOU IN

Scripture:
"For my father and mother have forsaken me, but the Lord will take me in."

Psalm 27:10 ESV

Explanation:
Being forgotten by your parents can hurt you physically, emotionally, and even mentally. But the good news is that even if your parents ever abandoned you or put you up for adoption, God has always loved you and called you His precious daughter. When you accepted God into your heart and made Jesus your Lord and Savior, God adopted you into His family of believers. Because of your faith in Jesus, you get to be with Him in heaven forever when your assignment on earth is done.

Bedtime Prayer:

Dear God, thank you for accepting me into your family. Amen.

DAY 211: IN GOD'S THOUGHTS

Scripture:
"How precious to me are your thoughts, O God..."

Psalm 139:18-19 ESV

Explanation:
You might wonder how a loving God could care about you so much. But He has loved and cared about you since He thought of and created you. His thoughts are way beyond your thoughts, and His thoughts towards you are precious. He considers you precious and only wants what is best for you. Ask Him to guide you on the right path. You are always on His mind. He is ready, willing, and able to help you make this world a better place for the good of His kingdom.

Bedtime Prayer:

Dear God, thank you for saying that I'm precious in your thoughts. Amen.

DAY 212: FATHER TO THE FATHERLESS

Scripture:
"Father of the fatherless..."

Psalm 68:5 ESV

Explanation:
You may not have grown up with a father. But there is a person who truly wants to be your father. That person is Jesus. He wants to be a father to you when your earthly father isn't there for you. You can count on Him in ways you may not have been able to count on your earthly father. He is always there for you, never stops loving you, and wraps His loving arms around you. He is always there to listen to you no matter what.

Bedtime Prayer:

Dear God, thank you for being my heavenly Father. Amen.

DAY 213: THE LORD STANDS BY YOU

Scripture:
"But the Lord stood by me and strengthened me..."

2 Timothy 4:17 ESV

Explanation:
Whenever you doubt your ability to go on, God stands by you and sends the Holy Spirit and Jesus to comfort you. He gives you the strength you didn't think you had inside of you for each task ahead and gives you the courage to keep going. He stands by you every step of the way. He strengthens you with His everlasting strength. Hold on to His hands, and remember how He strengthened you before. He can and will always come through with strength for you again.

Bedtime Prayer:

Dear God, thank you for always standing by me and strengthening me. Amen.

DAY 214: GO SOMEWHERE PRIVATE TO PRAY

Scripture:
"But he would withdraw to desolate places and pray."

Luke 5:16 ESV

Explanation:
Praying is an important part of everyday life. Even Jesus would retreat to a quiet place and pray to His heavenly Father. He told God everything, even though God already knew everything about Him. You, too, can withdraw to a peaceful place and pray every day, especially when your heart feels weary and needs encouragement and peace. No matter where you pray, God hears you. Whether you say your prayers out loud or in the stillness of your heart, He always wants to hear from you.

Bedtime Prayer:

Dear God, thank you for reminding me to pray secretly. Amen.

DAY 215: NOTHING CAN SEPARATE US

Scripture:
"...nor anything else in all creation, will be able to separate us from the love of God..."

Romans 8:38-39 ESV

Explanation:
Nothing can or could ever separate you from the love of Jesus Christ, your Lord. Once you are saved, nothing in heaven or earth can take you away from God if you keep your faith strong. Nothing in all of creation will be able to separate you from God. Take comfort in the thought that you're never too far gone to return to God and ask Him to forgive you. No matter what you do, you aren't ever separated from God.

Bedtime Prayer:

Dear God, thank you that nothing can separate me from you. Amen.

DAY 216: CRUCIFY WORLDLY PASSIONS

Scripture:
"And those who belong to Christ Jesus have crucified the flesh with its passions and desires."

Galatians 5:24 ESV

Explanation:
What are worldly pleasures?" you might be asking. They are anything that takes your attention off furthering God's kingdom. But since you belong to Jesus Christ, you can crucify your earthly passions daily. Ask God to help you stay focused on Him instead of thinking about and dwelling on earthly passions like getting good grades, making the varsity sports team, and being seen as the best daughter. Those passions only make you think of yourself and remove your focus from God. He will help you focus on Him.

Bedtime Prayer:

Dear God, please help me to crucify my worldly passions and worship only you. Amen.

DAY 217: LONGING FOR GOD

Scripture:
"My soul longs, yes, faints for the courts of the Lord…"

Psalm 84:2 ESV

Explanation:
There is nothing wrong with longing for time with God or being in His holy presence. Longing for God is a fantastic and incredible feeling. When you long for Him, He reaches His hands to you and pulls you out of the pit of despair that you're in. He refreshes your soul, mind, and body with His unexplainable peace. You might feel faint when you long for Him because you need to be rejuvenated by His presence. Go to Him and seek Him with everything you have.

Bedtime Prayer:
Dear God, I long for you every day. Help me stay close to you. Amen.

DAY 218: SINGING FOR GOD

Scripture:
"… my heart and flesh sing for joy to the living God."

Psalm 84:2 ESV

Explanation:
You might love to sing praises to Jesus at home, during Sunday school, or outdoors in nature. You are free and allowed to sing to Him whenever you want to. It doesn't matter how good or bad your voice is because God loves it when you sing His praises daily or weekly during church. Take every opportunity to sing His praises to Him because He truly deserves it. He is worthy of your praise. So sing to Him with everything you have, every chance you get.

Bedtime Prayer:
Dear God, please let me sing for you every day of my life. Amen.

DAY 219: WHOM HAVE I IN HEAVEN?

Scripture:
"Whom have I in heaven but you? And there is nothing on earth that I desire besides you."

Psalm 73:25 ESV

Explanation:
This verse might be confusing. But it reminds you that you have no one to turn to in heaven except Jesus. You have God in your life and on your side at all times. Your job on earth is to help as many people come to know Christ as possible. There is no one you should actively seek with all of your heart like Jesus. Jesus has to be your number one priority. After all, you get to be with Him in eternity.

Bedtime Prayer:
Dear God, I desire you. Thank you for giving me a place in heaven. Amen.

DAY 220: HUNGER AND THIRST FOR RIGHTEOUSNESS

Scripture:
"Blessed are those who hunger and thirst for righteousness, for they shall be satisfied."

Mathew 5:6 ESV

Explanation:
When you hunger and thirst, you usually get something to eat and drink. But what about when you hunger and thirst for righteousness? You can hunger and thirst for righteousness from God. He will give you everlasting water to drink by the power of the Holy Spirit. He will allow you to touch people's lives with His good news. God will ensure you're satisfied whenever you hunger and thirst for righteousness. He will help you know Him in new and exciting ways you never expected to experience.

Bedtime Prayer:
Dear God, please help me hunger and thirst for your righteousness. Amen.

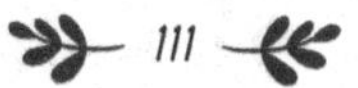

DAY 221: LOVE THE LORD

Scripture:

"You shall love the Lord your God with all your heart and with all your soul and with all your might."

Deuteronomy 6:5 ESV

Explanation:

"How can I love the Lord with all my heart, soul, and mind?" you might ask. You aren't the only kid who has asked that question. God wants you to do your best to honor, love, and respect Him as your Savior. That means thinking before you speak and act and reminding yourself to do your best not to sin daily. Love the Lord and honor Him by honoring your friends, family, classmates, coaches, and every other authority figure. Love God and others through your thoughts, words, and actions daily.

Bedtime Prayer:

Dear God, help me to love you with everything I have. Amen.

DAY 222: GOD IS LOVE

Scripture:

"Anyone who does not love does not know God, because God is love."

1 John 4:8 ESV

Explanation:

It might seem hard to believe, but not everyone knows, acknowledges, or loves God. Not everyone acknowledges God or wants to know Him personally. He sent Jesus to die on the cross for your sins and the sins of the whole world. That's the purest definition of love: laying down your life for someone you love. God is love, not just because of Him sacrificing His Son Jesus, but because Jesus died to take your punishment away and give you an eternal home with Him in heaven.

Bedtime Prayer:

Dear God, please help me love everyone as you do. Amen.

DAY 223: GOD SHOWS COMPASSION

Scripture:
"As a father shows compassion to his children, so the Lord shows compassion to those who fear him."

Psalm 103:13 ESV

Explanation:
When did your dad last show compassion towards you by hugging or congratulating you for scoring a game-winning goal? God shows you even more compassion than your dad because God loves you even more than your earthly dad could. He shows His love toward you daily with blessings such as the ability to wake up, walk, talk, see, play sports, and spend time with your family. God doesn't want you to fear Him but rather embrace His never-ending love towards you. God is always compassionate towards you.

Bedtime Prayer:
Dear God, thank you for showing me your compassion. Amen.

DAY 224: WAITING TO BE GRACIOUS

Scripture:
"Therefore the Lord waits to be gracious to you..."

Isaiah 30:18 ESV

Explanation:
You will not always want to be good and gracious to everyone. You will not always want to forgive those who hurt you immediately, but think of it this way: Since God is so gracious towards you, how can you not be gracious to anyone else? How can you not forgive someone else when God's already forgiven you for your mistakes? God waits every second of every day, wanting to be gracious and to bestow His blessings upon you as His child. He never wants to see you falter.

Bedtime Prayer:
Dear God, thank you for always being ready to be gracious to me. Amen.

DAY 225: COVENANT OF PEACE

Scripture:
"... my covenant of peace shall not be removed..."

Isaiah 54:10 ESV

Explanation:
God's covenant of peace is everlasting and will never be removed. You can do nothing to get Him to remove His covenant of holy peace. You might wonder, "How will I know if I have a holy covenant of peace with God?" Here are ways to recognize it: you will feel peace beyond your understanding. You will feel calm amid stressful homework, tests, or stressful games. You will be able to focus when other kids can't concentrate. Ask Him to cover you with His covenant of peace.

Bedtime Prayer:

Dear God, thank you for your ever-lasting covenant of peace. Amen.

DAY 226: LOVE COVERS ALL

Scripture:
"Hatred stirs up strife, but love covers all offenses."

Proverbs 10:12 ESV

Explanation:
Have you ever told a family member or friend you hate them? How did you feel immediately following that encounter? You most likely felt guilty for saying mean and hurtful words that you couldn't take back. That's why God wants to remind you that hatred stirs up strife and conflict, but love covers all offenses. The sooner you apologize, the better it'll be for you. Nothing is worth saying, "I hate you." It's better to forgive. Let God's love cover all offenses between you and the other person.

Bedtime Prayer:

Dear God, thank you for covering all my offenses. Amen.

DAY 227: IN HIM, WE LIVE

Scripture:

"'In him we live and move and have our being."

Acts 17:28 ESV

Explanation:

In God, we live, move, and have our being. That means God is already inside you from the second you were born and baptized. He made you perfectly in His image and gave you specific talents to honor, love, and respect Him. He guides you on the correct path to take every day. You have to listen to His small, steady voice in the form of the Holy Spirit. Because He thought the world needed you, He's letting His excellent plan for your life play out. Live for Him!

Bedtime Prayer:

Dear God, thank you for allowing me to live and move because of you. Amen.

DAY 228: POWER OF YOUR TONGUE

Scripture:

"Death and life are in the power of the tongue..."

Proverbs 18:21 ESV

Explanation:

"What do people mean when they say life and death are in the power of the tongue? It means that even though the tongue is the smallest part of your body, you have the power of life and death flowing from your words. That's right. You can either build people up or tear people down with your words, thoughts, and actions. So the next time you want to say something nasty to someone, consider the consequences your words and actions could have on someone's life.

Bedtime Prayer:

Dear God, remind me that my words have the power to hurt and heal. Amen.

DAY 229: SWEETNESS TO THE SOUL

Scripture:
"Gracious words are like a honeycomb, sweetness to the soul and health to the body."

Proverbs 16:24 ESV

Explanation:
Do you like sweets like chocolate, candy, and ice cream? Have you ever tasted honey in a warm glass of tea? Gracious words are like a honeycomb, meaning they bring sweetness to someone's soul and health to their body. Wouldn't you rather be the one who gives life to someone's body and soul than someone who hurts others with your words? You can be like Jesus today and bring love, encouragement, prayers, and peace to everyone around you.

Bedtime Prayer:

Dear God, please help my words to bring sweetness to people's souls. Amen.

DAY 230: BE DOERS OF THE WORD

Scripture:
"But be doers of the word, and not hearers only."

James 1:22 ESV

Explanation:
You can be a doer of God's word and not just a hearer by sharing the love of Jesus with those who don't know Him yet. You can also be doers of His word by sharing His word with everyone you meet. Your actions can have a positive impact for generations to come. Be an encourager to your friends and family members who are struggling. Be there for them just as Jesus is there for you. Live for Jesus in all you say and do.

Bedtime Prayer:

Dear God, help me to be a doer of what I read in your word. Amen.

DAY 231: CARES OF MY HEART

Scripture:
"When the cares of my heart are many, your consolations cheer my soul."

Psalm 94:19 ESV

Explanation:
If you have ever felt like the weight of the world was crashing down on you, you aren't the only kid who has struggled. Jesus invites you to come to Him when things become too much and too heavy for you to bear on your own. He doesn't want you to carry that load on your own. Instead, pray and give it up to Him. He is strong enough to take it. When He lifts those worries from you, you will feel His unexplainable joy return to you.

Bedtime Prayer:

Dear God, thank you for cheering me up when life gets to me. Amen.

DAY 232: DON'T WORRY ABOUT TOMORROW

Scripture:
"Therefore, do not be anxious about tomorrow, for tomorrow will be anxious for itself."

Mathew 6:34 ESV

Explanation:
You might wonder, "How can I not worry about tomorrow?" But it's simple. God only wants you to focus on the seconds, minutes, and hours in front of you today. You can only control your feelings and reactions about today. Today is the only day you need to be concerned about. Don't burden yourself with thoughts of "Will I pass my math test tomorrow? Oh man, what'll happen tomorrow?" Those thoughts will only bring stress and negativity to your life. God wants to bring His peace to you every day.

Bedtime Prayer:

Dear God, please teach me that I don't need to worry about tomorrow. Amen.

DAY 233: EACH DAY HAS ITS PROBLEMS

Scripture:
"Sufficient for the day is its own trouble."

Mathew 6:34 ESV

Explanation:
God only gives you the mental, physical, and spiritual capacity to focus on one day at a time. He doesn't want you to constantly fear what could happen tomorrow because fear of the future takes away from the peace that you could and should be experiencing today. Every day has enough problems of its own. The good news is that God knows everything that will occur in your day and future. Trust Him and believe that He will work out everything for your good.

Bedtime Prayer:

Dear God, please help me focus only on today, not tomorrow. Amen.

DAY 234: GOD IS MY HELPER

Scripture:
".... The Lord is my helper; I will not fear; what can man do to me?"

Hebrews 13:6 ESV

Explanation:
No matter what happens, you can confidently say that the Lord is your helper, Savior, and Lord over your life. You can even say, "What can man do to me?" because it's true. Even though hard times will come upon your life, God will always give you a way out of, around, or through each hardship. You don't have to be scared when you know and believe without a shadow of a doubt that God got you through before, and you know He can do it again.

Bedtime Prayer:

Dear God, thank you. No one can harm me because you protect me. Amen.

DAY 235: A GOOD WORD FROM GOD

Scripture:
"Anxiety in a man's heart weighs him down, but a good word makes him glad."

Proverbs 12:25 ESV

Explanation:
Anxiety can creep its way into your heart and mind at any time. Remember that anxiety can easily weigh your heart down and make you doubt yourself and your abilities. When you tire of carrying your thoughts around, lift them to God. He is strong enough to take them. When you're weighed down with anxiety, ask for a good word from God. He will send the right people to encourage you and help you see how blessed you are. Then, you can inspire others in the same way.

Bedtime Prayer:

Dear God, please help me encourage people like you encourage me. Amen.

DAY 236: GOD DELIVERED ME

Scripture:
"I sought the Lord, and he answered me and delivered me from all my fears."

Psalm 34:4 ESV

Explanation:
Psalms is a beautiful book of prayers in the Bible, written mainly by King David. He went through many trials and tests, but God delivered David from them all. He will deliver you from all your troubles in school, on the sports team, at home, with friends or family. Call out to God whether it's day or night. He will answer with either a "yes" and change your situation, a "no" and help you grow through your trials, or "I have something better" to teach you to lean on Him.

Bedtime Prayer:

Dear God, help me to encourage anyone who has anxiety with your words. Amen.

DAY 237: PERFECT LOVE

Scripture:
"There is no fear in love, but perfect love casts out fear."

1 John 4:18 ESV

Explanation:
Only one person has perfect love for everyone on earth. That's God. God's love far outweighs everyone else's love on earth because His love saved you. His love sacrificed His one and only Son, Jesus, on the cross. Remember, there is no fear in love. There is no fear of punishment for you when you believe in God. God's love casts out all fear from your mind, soul, and body because He wants you to rest assured in Him and trust His perfect love and great plan for your life.

Bedtime Prayer:

Dear God, thank you for your perfect love that casts away my fear. Amen.

DAY 238: SUFFERING FOR GOD

Scripture:
"But even if you should suffer for righteousness' sake, you will be blessed."

1 Peter 3:14 ESV

Explanation:
When you're suffering, you can only think of how hard it is to escape that situation. You may doubt you'll get out of the problematic situation. Remember, when you get called names or made fun of for following Jesus, God will bless you. No matter what you go through on earth, your suffering for His name will be well worth it when you reach heaven. When you suffer for righteousness' sake, you are blessed because you're doing what He called you to do. You're telling others about Him.

Bedtime Prayer:

Dear God, thank you for blessing me when I suffer hardships in your name. Amen.

DAY 239: STRONGHOLD OF YOUR LIFE

Scripture:
"The Lord is the stronghold of my life; of whom shall I be afraid?"

Psalm 27:1 ESV

Explanation:
How often do you wallow in self-pity when facing difficulties? Feeling sorry for yourself for a few minutes is okay when upset. But don't stay in that mindset. Instead, declare, "The Lord is the stronghold of my life. Of whom shall I be afraid? He is in control of everything." When you declare that you get your strength from God, you declare His goodness, grace, love, and mercy over every area of your life. Saying God's promises out loud will help you have a positive life.

Bedtime Prayer:

Dear God, give me strength. Please help me not to be scared in school. Amen.

DAY 240: DON'T DREAD THEM

Scripture:
"...Do not fear or be in dread of them..."

Deuteronomy 31:6 ESV

Explanation:
You might think your bullies will always scare you into submitting to them, but you don't have to fear them because God is with you. He is on your side. He is with you on the playground, in the hallways, and in sports practice when they taunt you with mean words. Please don't give into the fear or dread of them. Don't give fear a place in your mind or heart. Instead, ask God to provide you with the courage and strength to face the bullies at school with no fear.

Bedtime Prayer:

Dear God, thanks for telling me not to be afraid of bullies in school. Amen.

DAY 241: BE CONTENT WITH WHAT YOU HAVE

Scripture:

"Keep your life free from love of money, and be content with what you have..."

Hebrews 13:5 ESV

Explanation:

If you find a good job when you're older, money and the joy it can bring you will solve your problems. That couldn't be farther from the truth. God wants you to free yourself from the love of money, no matter how old or young you are. He wants you to realize how blessed you are and be content with everything you have, like a loving family and friends, the ability to learn, and, most importantly, your relationship with Him as your Lord and Savior.

Bedtime Prayer:

Dear God, please help me to be content with every gift you give me. Amen.

DAY 242: YOU'RE NOT AN ORPHAN

Scripture:

"I will not leave you as orphans; I will come to you."

John 14:18 ESV

Explanation:

Many children suffer with no parents to guide them and give them the love they desperately need. Hopefully, you have a loving family. You might have a friend or two who were adopted, or you were adopted yourself. You were adopted into God's family as soon as you accepted His salvation. He says He will never leave you as an orphan. He will come to you and take you into His loving arms, giving you all the love and compassion you'll ever need.

Bedtime Prayer:

Dear God, thank you for not making me an orphan. Thank you for adopting me. Amen.

DAY 243: DON'T REBEL

Scripture:
"God settles the solitary in a home... but the rebellious dwell in a parched land."

Psalm 68:6 ESV

Explanation:
As you get older, the rules your parents put into place can start to drive you crazy. You'll want more independence. So you might rebel against them. God warns you not to rebel because it can lead to dangerous and deadly consequences. He wants you to obey your parents' rules no matter how strict or stupid they seem. Rebelling doesn't get you anywhere. However, obeying rules helps you become wiser. Rebelling may be fun for a night, but the consequences can last a lifetime.

Bedtime Prayer:

Dear God, teach me never to rebel against you or my parents. Amen.

DAY 244: A DOOR NO ONE CAN SHUT

Scripture:
"Behold, I have set before you an open door, which no one is able to shut..."

Revelation 3:8 ESV

Explanation:
Do you believe God can open doors that no one can shut? That's what God wants you to know from this verse. He is there with you when you're trying your best on a test in school multiple times but still fail. He will eventually open the door to help you pass the test. If you struggle to make friends, He will give you the right Christlike friends in His timing. He can and will open doors in every area of your life that no one can shut.

Bedtime Prayer:

Dear God, thank you for opening a door in my life that no one can shut. Amen.

DAY 245: NEVER DENY GOD

Scripture:
"I know that you have but little power, and yet you.... have not denied my name."

Revelation 3:8 ESV

Explanation:
God knows that you will fall and fail at times. But rest assured, He knew what would go wrong before you did. He knows you don't have enough power to get through life alone, so He gives you some of His everlasting power. He smiles when you keep His name sacred, even with the hard times you go through in school and life. Do your best never to deny Him or fall away from Him because He is the most essential part of your life.

Bedtime Prayer:

Dear God, thank you for never leaving me to fend for myself. Amen.

DAY 246: DON'T LOSE YOUR SOUL

Scripture:
"For what will it profit a man if he gains the whole world and forfeits his soul?"

Mathew 16:26 ESV

Explanation:
You will hear stories telling you it's okay to be a Christian and still have fun. You might think doing certain things is ok when they will only hurt you in the long run, like hanging with the wrong crowd, learning to steal, or talking back to authority figures. God asks you what it profits you to gain the world but lose your soul. Wouldn't you instead do what's right in God's eyes and spend eternity in heaven doing the right thing instead of the wrong worldly things?

Bedtime Prayer:

Dear God, please help me live my life fully dedicated to you daily. Amen

DAY 247: HEALED BY HIS WOUNDS

Scripture:
"By his wounds you have been healed."

1 Peter 2:24 ESV

Explanation:
Have you ever heard the Bible verse "By his wounds you have been healed"? It's true because, through His death on the cross, Jesus saved your life. By His wounds, you were healed and made a completely new human being and a child of the most high God. He loved you so much He sacrificed Himself so you could live with Him forever in heaven. You are free from sin through the nail marks in His hands and feet and the sphere piercing His side.

Bedtime Prayer:

Dear God, whenever I feel upset, remind me that your wounds heal me. Amen.

DAY 248: LONELY AND AFFLICTED

Scripture:
"Turn to me and be gracious to me, for I am lonely and afflicted."

Psalm 25:16 ESV

Explanation:
Have you ever cried out to God, asking for His help? Have you ever felt so lonely and afflicted (troubled) with pain? There is nothing wrong with crying out to God for deliverance from your pain and loneliness. Ask Him to turn toward you and be gracious, relieving your pain. Ask Him to help you bring His peace to others who are lonely and afflicted. See where He leads you. Impact the lives of others who are struggling. Encourage them that God will help them just like He helps you.

Bedtime Prayer:

Dear God, help me be gracious toward people like you are gracious towards me. Amen.

DAY 249: SUFFERING BE GLORIFIED IN HIM

Scripture:
"...we suffer with him in order that we may also be glorified with him."

Romans 8:17 ESV

Explanation:
Your suffering will not last forever, even though it will sometimes feel like it will never go away. God suffers with you whenever you go through troubles. Your pain and suffering are never in vain because God is allowing some of that pain to teach you to rely on Him instead of on your strength. You're suffering with Him and for His namesake so that He will get the praise, glory, honor, and respect He deserves. He wants to glorify you for your steadfast faith.

Bedtime Prayer:
Dear God, thank you for glorifying me through you whenever I suffer. Amen.

DAY 250: LET GOD'S PRESENCE BE WITH YOU

Scripture:
"And he said, "My presence will go with you, and I will give you rest."

Exodus 33:14 ESV

Explanation:
Whenever you start to feel overwhelmed in life, take a step back, take a deep breath, and realize just how blessed you are. Let God know what you're struggling with, and give your worries to Him. Allow Him to come into your daily life, especially when you feel like giving up. He will give you peace and rest and relieve all of your stress. Surround yourself with His presence every day. Allow yourself to rest in His calming presence when life feels too much to take.

Bedtime Prayer:
Dear God, thank you for letting me feel your presence and for giving me rest. Amen.

DAY 251: BROUGHT OUT OF YOUR DISTRESS

Scripture:
"The troubles of my heart are enlarged; bring me out of my distresses."

Psalm 25:17 ESV

Explanation:
God will care for you in every way, shape, and form. Whenever you're troubled, turn to God and ask Him to give you a way out of, around, and through every obstacle. When you need God the most, He is only a prayer away. He got you through your most challenging times before, and He will do it again, without a doubt. He will bring you out of your distress. Take His hand and let Him lead you back to physical, emotional, mental, and spiritual safety.

Bedtime Prayer:

Dear God, bring me out of my distress no matter what is causing me to suffer. Amen.

DAY 252: LIFE THROUGH JESUS CHRIST

Scripture:
"Whoever has the Son has life..."

1 John 5:12 ESV

Explanation:
This verse might scare you because it says whoever knows God as the Father and the Son has life. But many people in your home life, church, and community don't fully understand God. Therefore, they don't have life. But you can be Jesus' example for those people and help them realize that a relationship with Him is the best option in the world. Jesus can, has, and will save your life and the lives of people you talk to about Him.

Bedtime Prayer:

Dear God, allow me to know you and have life through you. Amen.

DAY 253: CONTINUALLY WITH YOU

Scripture:
"Nevertheless, I am continually with you; you hold my right hand."

Psalm 73:22 ESV

Explanation:
God is continually with you. Let that fact sink in. No matter what you're doing in school, on the sports field, or at home, He is always with you. God wants to be close to you. You're His precious child. He holds you in His hands every day and protects you from harm. But the distractions of life can get in the way of your relationship with God. He welcomes you back with open arms at all times. Just grab hold of His hand and ask Him to help you.

Bedtime Prayer:
Dear God, thank you for allowing me to hold your right hand. Amen.

DAY 254: ANOTHER HELPER

Scripture:
"And I will ask the Father, and he will give you another Helper, to be with you forever..."

John 14:16 ESV

Explanation:
God cares about every aspect of your life. He is there to help you at every step. He asked His heavenly Father to send you another helper in the form of the Holy Spirit. He promised His 12 disciples the Holy Spirit would be with them forever. He makes the same promise to you. The Holy Spirit is always with you, ready to help you at a moment's notice. Never forget that the still, small voice you hear is the Holy Spirit talking to you.

Bedtime Prayer:
Dear God, please help me know what you're teaching me as my helper. Amen.

DAY 255: ASKING GOD WHY

Scripture:
"My God, my God, why have you forsaken me?"

Mathew 27:46 ESV

Explanation:
Sometimes, you feel God abandoned you because of your sins. That could be farther from the truth. No matter what you do, God loves you and will never leave you. Jesus even felt like God had forsaken Him while He was dying on the cross on Good Friday. But then, God rose Him from the dead on that glorious Easter morning. Even though it feels like He has forgotten about you, He is preparing you for the ultimate victory through Jesus Christ.

Bedtime Prayer:

Dear God, thank you for never forsaking me, even when I feel alone. Amen

DAY 256: GOD HEARS YOU

Scripture:
"The Lord hears and delivers them out of all their troubles."

Psalm 34:19 ESV

Explanation:
God is not deaf or immune to your prayers and pleas. He hears every word you cry in the stillness of your heart and out loud. The Lord will get you out of harm's way. He hears your cries for deliverance. He delivered you from troubles before, and He will do it again. He is always there with you in the trenches of your situation, and He cries when you cry and celebrates with you when He gets you out of challenging situations. He wants you to be happy.

Bedtime Prayer:

Dear God, thank you for always listening to me. Amen.

DAY 257: HIS DISCIPLES

Scripture:
"... my Father is glorified, that you bear much fruit and so prove to be my disciples."

John 15:8 ESV

Explanation:
Being God's disciple is not for the faint of heart. It is not an easy thing to do when you're constantly persecuted for believing in God. Following God will give you enemies on earth. But, when you stand up for your faith and proclaim that Jesus is your Savior, God is automatically glorified. Whatever you do will be blessed even if you're being persecuted for your choice to be His disciple because it's through your words and actions that many more people will also come to be His disciples.

Bedtime Prayer:

Dear God, thank you for helping me lead others to be your disciples. Amen.

DAY 258: WHY DO YOU DOUBT

Scripture:
"O you of little faith, why did you doubt?"

Mathew 14:31 ESV

Explanation:
When you doubt, you let negativity and "what if" thoughts plague you. Have you ever had the question "Why do you doubt?" in your mind? That's the Holy Spirit whispering to you to start trusting God in every circumstance. Jesus asked His disciples why they doubted He could save them when they were in a storm on the Sea of Galilee. He asks you the same question whenever you doubt His perfect plan. Instead of doubting Him, look at all He has proven and everything He has gotten you through.

Bedtime Prayer:

Dear God, help me not doubt your power or presence. Amen.

DAY 259: GIVER OF COMFORT

Scripture:
"Blessed be the God and Father...the Father of mercies and God of all comfort."

2 Corinthians 1:3 ESV

Explanation:
Losing people you love can be one of the hardest things. You might seek comfort in the arms of your friends and other family members. But God is the main one you should be turning to. He will give you the strength to go on and continue to live the life He has called you to live. God is the God of mercies and the God of all comfort. Call on Him whenever you need comfort and fall into His loving arms.

Bedtime Prayer:

Dear God, thank you for providing me with your comfort and mercy. Amen.

DAY 260: YOU ARE HIS

Scripture:
"Fear not, for I have redeemed you; I have called you by name, you are mine."

Isaiah 43:1 ESV

Explanation:
Do you believe that you are His? The Bible says not to fear because God has redeemed you by your faith in Jesus Christ as your Lord and Savior. He has called you by name, and you are His. He chose you as His even before you were born and continually chooses you even when you make mistakes. How does that make you feel, knowing that God chose you and you are His forever? God called you by your name, one of His chosen daughters. Jesus died to save you.

Bedtime Prayer:

Dear God, thank you for making me your child. Amen.

DAY 261: DON'T DOUBT

Scripture:
"But let him ask in faith, with no doubting…"

James 1:6 ESV

Explanation:
Doubt can plague your mind at any time. You might doubt your abilities in school, sports teams, or helping others know Christ. You might even doubt yourself when your parents talk down your dreams or when a friend of yours makes fun of you for being a Christian. But God encourages you to walk tall and stand firm in your faith without letting doubt plague your sense of worth. God loves it when you stand tall among any doubts, praising His name and helping others know Him personally.

Bedtime Prayer:
Dear God, please help me to believe in you and not doubt your plan. Amen.

DAY 262: BELIEVE GOOD THINGS WILL HAPPEN

Scripture:
"…. 'Be taken up and thrown into the sea,' it will happen."

Mathew 21:21 ESV

Explanation:
If you believe and keep your faith strong while doing what God has told you, you will see the fruits of your faith come to pass. Because of your faith, God will allow good things to happen. Many of your friends and family will come to know Jesus as their Savior. This verse says that Jesus told His disciples to believe that the mountain would be thrown into the sea if they believed in Him. Believe that good things will continually happen in your life without doubt in your heart.

Bedtime Prayer:
Dear God, please help me believe that good things will happen through my faith. Amen.

DAY 263: WHY ARE YOU TROUBLED?

Scripture:
"Why are you troubled, and why do doubts arise in your hearts?"

Luke 24:38 ESV

Explanation:
Whenever you're afraid, ask yourself why you feel troubled. It's most likely because of the uncertainty of whether things will work out how you want. God asks you the same thing in your mind and heart daily, but it's up to you to listen to His Holy Spirit's leading. You don't need to let doubt arise in your heart because you have a God on your side who always can, always has, and always will do all things for your good and the good of His glory.

Bedtime Prayer:

Dear God, help my heart not to be troubled. Focus my heart on you. Amen.

DAY 264: HAVE MERCY ON THE DOUBTER

Scripture:
"And have mercy on those who doubt..."

Jude 1:22 ESV

Explanation:
God knows you will eventually doubt His plans for your life. But He will turn all your doubt into a message and testimony of how He was glorified through your life. Then, you can help others who doubt God's plan for their life. Your testimony can be the turning point for your friends, family, and even complete strangers believing in God. When you experience doubters of God's truth, have mercy on any doubters. Have mercy on them, just like how God has mercy on you when you doubt.

Bedtime Prayer:

Dear God, please have mercy on me when I start doubting you. Amen.

DAY 265: DON'T BE DOUBTING THOMAS

Scripture:
"Put your finger here... see my hands... put out your hand... place it in my side..."

John 20:27 ESV

Explanation:
Everyone has doubted God and His message at one time in their lives. Hopefully, you don't doubt whether Jesus rose from the grave on Easter morning. But Thomas, one of the 12 disciples, doubted Jesus rose to life. He said, "Unless I put my hands in the nail marks in His hands and put my hand in His side, I won't believe. Then Jesus appeared to Him and asked Thomas to feel His hands with the nail marks and place his hands on Jesus' side. Talk about an eye-opener.

Bedtime Prayer:

Dear God, please help me not to doubt you as Thomas did. Help me believe. Amen.

DAY 266: BELIEVE IN WHAT YOU CAN'T SEE

Scripture:
"Do not disbelieve, but believe."

John 20:27 ESV

Explanation:
It can be hard to believe in God, especially when you can't physically see Him like His disciples could. But He gave the same message to you- don't disbelieve, but believe. He wants you to believe in Him at all times. You can still feel His holy presence even when you can't see Him. He whispers in your ear the right and wrong things to do to help others believe in Him the way you do. Give them the hope to believe in the God they don't see.

Bedtime Prayer:

Dear God, help me to believe in you even when I can't see you.

DAY 267: HELP MY UNBELIEF

Scripture:
"Immediately, the father of the child cried out and said, "I believe; help my unbelief!"

Mark 9:24 ESV

Explanation:
In the Bible, there was a father whose child had an unclean spirit. Jesus asked how long the son had the impure spirit. The father said since birth. The father wanted Jesus to heal his son and said, "If you can do anything, have compassion on us..." Jesus asked, "If you can? All things are possible with God." From that moment on, the boy was cleansed of the unclean spirit. The father cried, "I believe! Help my unbelief." Jesus invites you to ask Him to help your unbelief, too.

Bedtime Prayer:

Dear God, I boldly ask you to "help my unbelief." Amen.

DAY 268: BELIEVE THAT HE EXISTS

Scripture:
"...whoever would draw near to God must believe that he exists..."

Hebrews 11:6 ESV

Explanation:
When you started believing in God, you had to believe He exists fully. What can you do to help yourself believe that He is real? You begin to feel His promises when you draw near to Him daily. Read His word. You can attend a children's bible study or church every week. Praying helps you know Him more. Ask God to show you physical signs that He's real, like the color of a sunset, the beauty of a rainstorm, or a friend being there for you.

Bedtime Prayer:

Dear God, help me believe you're here and tell others you exist. Amen.

DAY 269: GOD HEARS YOUR PLEAS FOR HELP

Scripture:
"But you heard the voice of my pleas for mercy when I cried to you for help."

Psalm 31:22 ESV

Explanation:
God hears your pleas for help, whether you scream them out loud or keep them in your heart. He's never deaf to any of your feelings. He weeps with you when you weep. Jesus intercedes on your behalf, asking God to remove anything disturbing you. God hears you and wants to bring His everlasting peace, love, and happiness back into your heart, body, mind, and soul. Never stop calling out to Him for mercy and His guidance because He is making moves to guide you every step of the way.

Bedtime Prayer:
Dear God, thank you for hearing my cries and pleas for help daily. Amen.

DAY 270: HEARING GOD'S WORD

Scripture:
"So faith comes from hearing, and hearing through the word of Christ."

Romans 10:17 ESV

Explanation:
Where can I go to hear God's word? you might ask. You can ask your family to tell you about God and help you understand what you read in His word. You can also go to a children's Bible study or a group called Children's church where the Sunday school teacher preaches the same sermon taught in church but at your appropriate age level. Faith comes from hearing and hearing by listening to others talk about Jesus.

Bedtime Prayer:
Dear God, please help strengthen my faith by hearing your words. Amen.

DAY 271: SOME PEOPLE DOUBT

Scripture:
"And when they saw him, they worshiped him, but some doubted."

Mathew 28:17 ESV

Explanation:
There are a lot of Christians in this world. You might ask how anyone can doubt God's truth or His goodness. Some people indeed doubt God and His Son Jesus because they can't see Him, or they're going through a lot of difficulties and are unsure that He is truly there for them. But that's where you come in. You can tell them how Jesus has helped you through every step of your life. Tell others there's no reason to doubt Him because He never lets anyone down.

Bedtime Prayer:

Dear God, please help me to open the eyes of those who doubt you. Amen

DAY 272: GOD CALMS THE STORMS

Scripture:
"Then he rose and rebuked the winds and the sea, and there was a great calm."

Mathew 8:26 ESV

Explanation:
Sometimes God calms the storms in your life, and other times, He calms you in the middle of a storm. A massive storm arose when He and His disciples crossed the Sea of Galilee. The disciples were terrified, yet low and behold, Jesus was sleeping. Jesus got up and calmed the wind and the sea. Jesus calms you in the middle of storms in your life, too. When you think you can't make it, Jesus brings you through the storm or calms the storm in your life.

Bedtime Prayer:

Dear God, thank you for calming the storms of life and for calming me. Amen.

DAY 273: CALL ON GOD DURING TROUBLE

Scripture:

"And call upon me in the day of trouble; I will deliver you, and you shall glorify me."

Psalm 50:15 ESV

Explanation:

How many times a day do you call on God during trouble at school? Maybe you struggle to make baskets during practice for a big game or understand math, history, or science before a big test. Don't fret. God's got your back, and He will help you make the baskets, layups, and passes before the big game, and He will help you understand each subject before the tests. Just call out to Him and He will deliver you from your troubles. Then you'll get to glorify Him.

Bedtime Prayer:

Dear God, thanks for letting me call upon you during tough times. Amen.

DAY 274: BELIEVE IN HIM EVEN WHEN YOU DON'T SEE HIM

Scripture:

"Blessed are those who have not seen and yet have believed."

John 20:29 ESV

Explanation:

Many people struggle to believe in God because they can't physically see Him. But God wants you to help them understand what fully believing in Him means. You can explain that you don't see God yet but know He is always present. Then you can explain that those who believe in God even though they can't see Him are blessed. God will bless you when you believe in His plan for your life, even when you can't see Him.

Bedtime Prayer:

Dear God, show me how to help other people's unbelief. Amen.

DAY 275: BAPTISM STRENGTHENS YOUR FAITH

Scripture:
"Whoever believes and is baptized will be saved, but whoever does not believe will be condemned."

Mark 16:16 ESV

Explanation:
Kids your age might be very curious about baptism. If you've been baptized, you can explain the excitement and awe of being cleansed of all your sins and beginning a new relationship with Jesus as your Savior. You get dunked into the tub of water in the name of the Father, Son, and Holy Spirit. Then, you come out of the water, a new person on fire for the Lord. Being baptized and becoming a child of God saves your life.

Bedtime Prayer:

Dear God, help me to show others how awesome it is to be baptized. Amen.

DAY 276: MARVELING AT PEOPLE'S UNBELIEF

Scripture:
"And he marveled because of their unbelief. And he went about among the villages teaching."

Mark 6:6 ESV

Explanation:
If you see people struggling in their faith walk, ask God to help you know what to do and say to them. There will be many people who will not believe in Him for many different reasons. You can try to change their mind about believing in God, and some people's reasons for not believing in God may shock you. Jesus even marveled at people's unbelief, but He went on teaching them anyhow. You can do the same thing He did. Help make an impact on the world.

Bedtime Prayer:

Dear God, please tell me how I can help those struggling with faith. Amen.

DAY 277: WHATEVER WE ASK, WE RECEIVE

Scripture:

"And whatever we ask we receive from him, because we... do what pleases him."

1 John 3:22 ESV

Explanation:

You might ask your parents if you will receive what you ask for if you do your best to please the Lord. It really is true. If you consistently think about your words and actions and whether or not they please God, you'll work to please Him. If the things you do and say don't please God, you must change your ways. Whatever you ask for, you will receive it from Him because you do and say things that please Him.

Bedtime Prayer:

Dear God, please help me to believe that whatever I ask, I'll receive from you. Amen.

DAY 278: DON'T GET OFFENDED BY GOD

Scripture:

"And blessed is the one who is not offended by me."

Mathew 11:6 ESV

Explanation:

Are there people who are offended by God and offended by people talking about God? Yes, those people exist. But just because someone you know gets offended by your Christian attitude and your passion for talking about your faith doesn't mean you have to stop talking about Jesus. Remember, the people offended by Jesus need Him most in their lives. So, instead of being offended by them, pray for them to come to know Christ instead.

Bedtime Prayer:

Dear God, please help me never to be offended by you. Amen.

DAY 279: YOU HAVE ETERNAL LIFE

Scripture:
"I write these things to you who believe in the name of the Son of God..."

1 John 5:13 ESV

Explanation:
Isn't it a great feeling to know that you're saved by your faith in Jesus Christ as your Savior? That means that as soon as you professed your faith in God and asked Him to forgive your sins, He forgave, accepted, and welcomed you as His child. Through your faith, you now have eternal life, which means you get the most incredible gift—a spot in heaven for all eternity and the ability to call on God at any time, day or night.

Bedtime Prayer:
Dear God, thank you for giving me eternal life. Amen.

DAY 280: BE STILL AND KNOW

Scripture:
"Be still, and know that I am God."

Psalm 46:10 ESV

Explanation:
When you struggle in life, you might ask yourself, "How can I be still and know that you're God?" It's simple. Jesus wants you to give everything you are feeling up to Him. Let Him go to work on it instead of wasting your energy. He invites you to share your worries and concerns with Him and be still in His presence. Let your shoulders relax, and let your muscles unclench. He wants you to know and trust He has you in His hands.

Bedtime Prayer:
Dear God, thank you for teaching me to be still in your presence. Amen.

DAY 281: GOD CREATED YOU

Scripture:
"...male and female he created them."

Genesis 1:27 ESV

Explanation:
God created you with many unique abilities, skills, and talents that no one else has. No one else has your love, light, laughter, smile, peace, faith, family, or fingerprint. Just like God created you as a girl, God also created boys. He made them with abilities and talents that girls don't have. Likewise, girls have many skills that boys don't have. Embrace your body. Be proud to stand up for your faith. Be the girl He created you to be.

Bedtime Prayer:

Dear God, thank you for making me unique and different than everyone else. Amen.

DAY 282: GOD'S WAY OF SPEAKING TO YOU

Scripture:
"All Scripture is breathed out by God and profitable for teaching, for reproof, for correction..."

2 Timothy 3:16 ESV

Explanation:
God points out His ways of correcting you throughout His word. He wants you to be trained and know how you should and shouldn't act. He also wants you to see the difference between right and wrong in any situation. All scripture is thought out and breathed out by God Himself. Reading and studying it daily and weekly is essential for proper teaching. You also get the important reproof and correction of your ways throughout your life.

Bedtime Prayer:

Dear God, thank you for pointing out your ways of correcting me. Amen

DAY 283: HE KNOWS YOU

Scripture:

"Before I formed you in the womb I knew you..."

Jeremiah 1:5 ESV

Explanation:

God knows you and knew you before He even created you. He knew His plan for your life before He created you. He knows you better than your parents, grandparents, siblings, extended family, friends, and pets. He knows you better than you know yourself. That's how much you can trust Him and His plan for your life. He knows exactly what will happen and when throughout your life. He knows all of your hopes, dreams, tears, and fears.

Bedtime Prayer:

Dear God, thank you for knowing me before birth. Amen.

DAY 284: IN THE BEGINNING

Scripture:

"In the beginning was the Word, and the Word was with God, and the Word was God."

John 1:1 ESV

Explanation:

God created the world, the sun, the sky, the creepy crawling bugs like spiders, beetles, and snakes. He made the oceans, the sand and the land, seashells, and all the creatures in the oceans. He created all animals that swim in the water and walk on land. Then He created man and woman. All He had to do was speak a single word, and everything came to be as God proclaimed it would be. The word was God because God spoke and created everything.

Bedtime Prayer:

Dear God, please help me to teach others about you by read-ing your word. Amen

DAY 285: BE A SERVANT EVEN WHEN IT'S DIFFICULT

Scripture:

"As each has received a gift, use it to serve one another..."

1 Peter 4:10-11 ESV

Explanation:

Everyone has unique gifts that they can use to glorify God and make a difference in this world—even you. Even though there will be times when you may not want to serve others, ask God to change your mindset. You might be tired, stressed from school, and not wanting to be nice to someone who hurt you, but use your gifts to serve them with a grateful heart anyhow. Try to make a difference even when you don't feel like it.

Bedtime Prayer:

Dear God, thank you for teaching me to serve people like you. Amen.

DAY 286: DON'T GIVE IN TO PEER PRESSURE

Scripture:

"My son, do not walk in the way with them; hold back your foot from their paths."

Proverbs 1:15 ESV

Explanation:

As fun as doing things with friends can seem, ask yourself, "Am I honoring God and keeping myself safe by doing this? Or am I willingly giving in to peer pressure?" Ways to know you're giving into peer pressure include an uneasy feeling in your mind and in your stomach, knowing what you're about to do is wrong, yet thinking it's not a big deal. Peer pressure can change your life in negative ways. You can stand tall in your faith when God tells you what to do.

Bedtime Prayer:

Dear God, please help me stand tall against peer pressure. Amen.

DAY 287: SOUL OF THE DILIGENT

Scripture:
"The soul of the sluggard craves and gets nothing, while the soul of the diligent is richly supplied."

Proverbs 13:4 ESV

Explanation:
When you do your best to be diligent in your daily faith walk, your life and soul will be richly supplied. Don't be a sluggish child because a sluggish person craves and gets nothing worthwhile. But the soul of the diligent is richly supplied. When you diligently use your faith to share the good news and how Jesus impacts your life, God will diligently bless you in many different ways. You could end up changing the world through your faith.

Bedtime Prayer:

Dear God, please help me to be diligent in everything I do. Amen.

DAY 288: MERE TALK

Scripture:
"In all toil there is profit, but mere talk tends only to poverty."

Proverbs 14:23 ESV

Explanation:
In every circumstance, there's toil, stress, anger, disappointment, sadness, and all other emotions combined. As bad as you might have a dream to accomplish something, just talking about it and not doing anything to achieve and make your dream a reality is only leading you to not only physical poverty but also spiritual, emotional, and mental poverty. If you don't go after your dreams, you're not taking action and proving what you can with God on your side. Don't just talk about your dreams. Act on them.

Bedtime Prayer:

Dear God, help me make life strides, not just talk about making them. Amen.

DAY 289: DON'T GRUMBLE

Scripture:
Do everything without grumbling or disputing that you may be blameless and innocent children."

Philippians 2:14-15 ESV

Explanation:
You're a kid; of course, there will be times when you grumble about going to school, completing homework, studying for tests, doing chores, honoring your parents, getting along with your siblings, and keeping your room clean. But God wants you to try your best to do everything without grumbling or complaining so that you become a blameless child of God. Every time you stop complaining about something you need to do and do it joyfully, it is easier to get closer to God.

Bedtime Prayer:

Dear God, please help me to stop grumbling when my mom asks me to help her. Amen.

DAY 290: COMMIT YOUR WAYS TO GOD

Scripture:
"Commit your work to the Lord, and your plans will be established."

Proverbs 16:3 ESV

Explanation:
How often do you commit your life and plans to God daily? Committing yourself to God is very important. The next time you're given an assignment, homework, or a test by your teacher or asked to do a task by your parents, stop for a moment. Pray for wisdom to know how to do the task, assignment, homework, or test to the best of your ability. Commit your work to the Lord, and your plans will be established.

Bedtime Prayer:

Dear God, I commit my life to you. Establish your plans for my life. Amen.

DAY 291: SHINE HIS LIGHT

Scripture:
"In the same way, let your light shine before others..."

Mathew 5:16 ESV

Explanation:
No matter how old you are, it's your job to let your love for Jesus shine in every possible way. You can make a difference in people's lives by telling them the good news and how Jesus can change their lives. Ask God how you can help your light shine before your friends, family, community, and church. He will lead you in the best ways to shine His light throughout your life and through your words and actions.

Bedtime Prayer:

Dear God, please help me shine your light among people. Amen.

DAY 292: GOD'S UNSEARCHABLE GREATNESS

Scripture:
"Great is the Lord, and greatly to be praised, and his greatness is unsearchable."

Psalm 145:3 ESV

Explanation:
God is great and worthy of being praised at all times. His greatness is unsearchable. You will never fully know how great He is because only God Himself knows how good He is. You can learn more about Him and His goodness in His Word through devotionals, Bible study, and by praying and praising Him. You can even get to know Him through having casual conversations about your life. Or you can ask Him what He wants you to do and patiently wait for His answer.

Bedtime Prayer:

Dear God, even though your greatness is unsearchable, help me know you better. Amen.

DAY 293: SING PRAISE WHETHER SAD OR GLAD

Scripture:
"Is anyone among you suffering? Let him pray. Is anyone cheerful? Let him sing praise."

James 5:13 ESV

Explanation:
Ask God to help you praise His name no matter how good or bad you feel this week. This verse says, "If anyone is suffering, pray for them and invite them to pray with you. Ask God to help them in the middle of their tough times." If you hear that a friend or family member is cheerful, thank God with them. Praise God with them through words, actions, and even through singing. Be cheerful when you need to be, and pray for those suffering.

Bedtime Prayer:

Dear God, help me sing your praise whether I'm sad or glad. Amen.

DAY 294: LIGHT IN THE DARKNESS

Scripture:
"The light shines in the darkness, and the darkness has not overcome it."

John 1:5 ESV

Explanation:
No matter what is going on in your life or how bleak things can get, you're never too far gone to be saved. God's love and light pierce through all darkness in your life. He allows you to see the light in the darkness and at the end of the tunnel. The darkness of sin will never overthrow the beauty of God's light. Nothing can stop God's light from pushing the darkness back to reveal His light and purpose for your life.

Bedtime Prayer:

Dear God, thank you for not allowing darkness to overcome your light. Amen.

DAY 295: IN GOD'S GLORY

Scripture:
"My mouth is filled with your praise, and with your glory all the day."

Psalm 71:8 ESV

Explanation:
Don't let anyone in school, your family, or your friend's group ever lead you in the wrong way of thinking. You can always worship God at any time, anywhere. No matter where you go or what you do, you are constantly in God's presence. Ask God to help you be less negative and more positive. Ask Him to reveal His goodness and why you should praise Him daily. Hopefully, you won't want to stop once you find reasons to glorify God.

Bedtime Prayer:

Dear God, please help me to glorify you all day, every day. Amen.

DAY 296: UNDERSTANDING TO THE SIMPLE

Scripture:
"The unfolding of your words gives light; it imparts understanding to the simple."

Psalm 119:130 ESV

Explanation:
Some people might think that salvation and faith in Jesus are too complicated for them, while others will say that they are too dirty to come before Him to ask for forgiveness. But God wants you to help them understand the simple and beautiful truth that anyone and everyone can be saved by professing that Jesus is their Lord and Savior, no matter what they've done. Ask Him how you can impart your wisdom so people can understand what God is trying to tell them.

Bedtime Prayer:

Dear God, thank you for allowing me to help people understand your simple yet essential truths. Amen.

DAY 297: CHILDREN OF LIGHT

Scripture:
"For you are all children of light, children of the day."

1 Thessalonians 5:5 ESV

Explanation:
You are the children of God's everlasting light and love. You're children of the day. Being a child of light means you can make drastic, Godly impacts in people's lives. Speak in love and tell them how Jesus can change their lives, how to start a personal relationship with Him, and how to make Him their Lord and Savior. Do all you can every day to reflect His light and be the person to lead people to Him.

Bedtime Prayer:

Dear God, thank you that I'm a child born again of your everlasting light. Amen.

DAY 298: WALK IN THE WAY OF THE LORD

Scripture:
"Blessed are those whose way is blameless, who walk in the law of the Lord!"

Psalm 119:1 ESV

Explanation:
Walking a blameless life as a child is not easy. So many distractions demand your attention that sometimes you might forget that you're sinning until after the fact. All you can do is ask Him for forgiveness, help you live a blameless life, and walk in Jesus' ways with Him at the forefront of it. There is nothing wrong with asking God for help to become more like Him. Do all you can to walk in His ways daily.

Bedtime Prayer:

Dear God, please help me to always walk in your ways throughout life. Amen.

DAY 299: BEARING WITNESS

Scripture:
"He came as a witness, to bear witness about the light, that all might believe through him."

John 1:7 ESV

Explanation:
Jesus is the best example of how to live a perfect and Godly life. No one other than Him is perfect. He came to this earth to witness and show everyone how meaningful a relationship with God is. Some people have listened to Him, and some others haven't. He bears witness by being the light of truth in this dark and confused world. Grab a hold of His hands, be His example, and walk in His everlasting light daily.

Bedtime Prayer:

Dear God, thank you for sending Jesus to bear witness to your light of pure truth. Amen.

DAY 300: THE LORD IS A LIGHT

Scripture:
"When I sit in darkness, the Lord will be a light to me."

Micah 1:7 ESV

Explanation:
As a kid, you're most likely afraid of the dark because you can't see what's in the dark. God wants you to be courageous instead of being scared. He wants you to know, believe, and declare that even though you sit and sleep in darkness, the Lord will be a beacon of light and hope. Declare, "I don't have to be afraid of the dark because God is protecting me as I sleep and when I rise to face each new day."

Bedtime Prayer:

Dear God, thank you for always being a light in any darkness in my life. Amen.

DAY 301: GENUINELY CONCERNED ABOUT YOU

Scripture:
"For I have no one like him, who will be genuinely concerned for your welfare."

James 2:20 ESV

Explanation:
Do you ever wonder who loves you the most in your family? Your parents and grandparents love you unconditionally. Your friends love you a ton, too, but there's one person who is always genuinely concerned about you. That's Jesus. He intercedes for you on your behalf, asking God to protect and take care of you, shield you from any harm, and give you a way out of temptation. He cared about your welfare so much that He died to provide you with a place in heaven.

Bedtime Prayer:
Dear God, thank you for being genuinely concerned about me. Amen.

DAY 302: OBEY GOD

Scripture:
"We must obey God rather than men."

Acts 5:29 ESV

Explanation:
Who do you want to obey the most in your life? You always want to follow your parents, grandparents, teachers, and coaches. But did you know obeying God is even more important than men? God is the main one who can lead you on the path of righteousness. Call on Him and ask Him to help you do the right thing according to His word, mercy, and grace. Ask Him to help you obey Him above everyone else in life.

Bedtime Prayer:
Dear God, help me to obey you rather than men. Amen.

DAY 303: PRAYING FAITH WON'T FAIL

Scripture:
"But I have prayed for you that your faith may not fail."

Luke 22:32 ESV

Explanation:
So many people in your life are praying that your faith stays strong. Your parents, siblings, grandparents, and extended family always want to see your faith strengthen and strengthen as you get older. They don't ever want to see your faith falter. It is a special thing to be prayed for, and it's an even bigger honor to pray that your friends and family's faith doesn't fail. Pray for their faith just like they pray for yours. Jesus smiles when you and others pray for strong faith.

Bedtime Prayer:

Dear God, thank you that people pray my faith won't fail. Amen.

DAY 304: GODLY GRIEF

Scripture:
"For godly grief produces a repentance that leads to salvation without regret..."

2 Corinthians 7:10 ESV

Explanation:
You might be wondering what Godly grief is. That kind of grief causes you pain but also brings much-needed hope to your heart. It reassures you that you are and will be forgiven for your sins. Ask God to help you repent quickly and not repeat the same mistakes. Godly grief leads to repentance, which strengthens your faith walk. Then, it leads to a better understanding of your salvation without regretting your past mistakes.

Bedtime Prayer:

Dear God, please help me to repent quickly. Amen.

DAY 305: TURN BACK

Scripture:
"Repent therefore, and turn back, that your sins may be blotted out"

Acts 3:19 ESV

Explanation:
Whenever you think you've done something that God can't forgive, you must remember that you are not that powerful. The only person who is that powerful is God. There is no sin that God won't forgive. You can always return to God and ask Him to change your heart and ways from the inside out. Turn back towards Him so that He can blot out your sins. When He sees you truly repenting and trying your hardest not to sin anymore, He forgives you automatically.

Bedtime Prayer:

Dear God, help me to turn back toward you. Amen.

DAY 306: GOD FORGETS YOUR SIN

Scripture:
"I will not remember your sins."

Isaiah 43:25 ESV

Explanation:
Doesn't it amaze you that God says He will not remember your sins anymore once you're forgiven? Knowing that your sins aren't held against you should bring you peace. It can also motivate you not to sin anymore. God casts your sin as far as the East is from the West. Knowing that God forgives and forgives your sins is a huge blessing. God forgets your sin but will never forget you as His child.

Bedtime Prayer:

Dear God, thank you for forgetting my sins. Amen.

DAY 307: DON'T BE ASHAMED OF FAITH

Scripture:
"if anyone suffers as a Christian, let him not be ashamed, let him glorify God in that name..."

1 Peter 4:19 ESV

Explanation:
Whenever you get made fun of for being a Christian and for professing your faith in Jesus Christ, don't be ashamed. The people who don't know God are trying to show you that your faith isn't important to them. Remember that people tend to mock things and people they don't understand. You can still proudly proclaim that Jesus is your Savior. Don't let anyone silence your faith. Be brave and tell people about Jesus no matter how people treat you.

Bedtime Prayer:
Dear God, help me never to be ashamed of my faith. Amen.

DAY 308: MOMENTARY AFFLICTION

Scripture:
"For this light momentary affliction is preparing for us an eternal weight of glory beyond all comparison..."

2 Corinthians 4:17 ESV

Explanation:
You might think the struggles you're going through with friends, as a cheerleader, sibling, daughter, granddaughter, and even as a Christian are hard to overcome. The important thing to remember is those struggles are nothing compared to the glory that awaits you in heaven. Once there, you will see God face to face in all His glory. All your troubles will be instantly forgotten, and you will feel peace beyond compre-hension. Instead of focusing on your problems, focus on the glory that awaits you in heaven.

Bedtime Prayer:
Dear God, help me to focus on the glory that awaits me in heaven. Amen.

DAY 309: WONDERFULLY MADE

Scripture:
"I praise you, for I am fearfully and wonderfully made..."

Psalm 139:14 ESV

Explanation:
Instead of looking at yourself in the mirror with pain and sorrow, look at yourself and say, "I'm God's holy and precious masterpiece. There is no one else like me. God made me unique and special." He fearfully and wonderfully made you. You never have to hate yourself because God will never hate you. Instead of being hard on yourself for how you look, talk, or dress, praise God for making you perfect just the way you are.

Bedtime Prayer:
Dear God, I praise you because I'm fearfully and wonderfully made. Amen.

DAY 310: WE ARE ALL THE SAME

Scripture:
"...for you are all one in Christ Jesus."

Galatians 3:28 ESV

Explanation:
You are made entirely different from everyone else. But when you and others are brothers and sisters in Christ, you are all one in Christ. We are all the same-we all sin every day. We all want to experience love and acceptance from the people in our lives. We all need forgiveness. You can do your best to accept people, whether or not they know God and despite the mistakes they make. We all make mistakes. We are all in need of a Savior.

Bedtime Prayer:
Dear God, please help me and others understand that we are all the same in Christ. Amen.

DAY 311: ONCE FAR OFF

Scripture:
"But now in Christ Jesus you who once were far off have been brought near..."

Ephesians 2:13 ESV

Explanation:
You sin daily, but God forgives you. No matter what you've done, He is always ready and willing to take you back in His loving, open arms. He never wants to cast you off. You can always come back to Him. He loves it when His children return home to Him, and you strengthen your faith. Because of Jesus' holy sacrifice on the cross, you were brought near to Him. Cling to Him with everything you've got because it's much better to be near God than far away.

Bedtime Prayer:

Dear God, thank you for bringing me near to you again. Amen.

DAY 312: REDEEMED THROUGH HIS BLOOD

Scripture:
"In him we have redemption through his blood, the forgiveness of our trespasses..."

Ephesians 1:7 ESV

Explanation:
When you accepted God into your life, you were redeemed and saved through the redemption of Jesus' blood and His death on the cross and resurrection. You are fully redeemed through the shedding of His holy precious blood. He forgives you for all your sins, including when you disobeyed your parents, yelled at your siblings, dishonored your coach, or didn't do your homework. No matter what you've done, you are saved, forgiven, and redeemed through Jesus' sacrifice. Isn't it amazing that He thought you were worth dying for?

Bedtime Prayer:

*Dear God, thank you for redeeming me through your blood.
Amen.*

DAY 313: BE HUMBLE BEFORE GOD

Scripture:

"Humble yourselves before the Lord, and he will exalt you."

James 4:10 ESV

Explanation:

Instead of bragging about your accomplishments, be humble. Don't brag about what you were able to do. Instead, acknowledge that you had Jesus' help to achieve good grades in school, be faster than others on the sports team, and how you made a difference in people's lives. All those things and more you will accomplish in your life are because of God's favor. Acknowledge that you only got to where you are today by God's mercy and grace. Humble yourself before God; when you reach heaven, He will exalt you.

Bedtime Prayer:

Dear God, please help me to be humble and honor you. Amen.

DAY 314: MORE VALUABLE

Scripture:

"Are you not of more value than they?

Mathew 6:26 ESV

Explanation:

You are more valuable than any other living creature on earth. Jesus tells you not to worry about anything because worrying can't add a single hour to your life. You're not trusting God enough if you're constantly worried about what you'll eat, drink, or your clothes. God tells you He takes care of the birds of the air. You are much more valuable than the birds; God knows exactly what you need before you even know it. He knows what you need before you even ask for it.

Bedtime Prayer:

Dear God, thank you for reminding me how valuable I am to you. Amen.

DAY 315: MAKING YOUR WAY PROSPEROUS

Scripture:
"then you will make your way prosperous, and then you will have good success."

Joshua 1:8 ESV

Explanation:
Knowing God and focusing on Him is the only way to succeed. If you want to succeed in school, at home, with your parents, in extracurricular activities, in church, and in getting along with your friends, siblings, and extended family, you must keep God at the center of your life. He is the only way you have had success before and the only way you will continue to succeed. When you keep your eyes on Him, He will make your ways prosperous and successful.

Bedtime Prayer:

Dear God, help me succeed by following you daily. Amen.

DAY 316: DON'T FORSAKE HIS STEADFAST LOVE

Scripture:
"Let not steadfast love and faithfulness forsake you..."

Proverbs 3:3 ESV

Explanation:
Ask God to comfort you when you feel lonely. He has always been and always will be by your side. He has never abandoned you, and He never will abandon you. Even with so many distractions, never forsake His love for you or think you can make it yourself. Without God, you won't be able to get very far in life. So turn to Him. Ask Him for guidance on how to love people the way He does and to be faithful to others the way He is faithful.

Bedtime Prayer:

Dear God, help me to keep your love and faithfulness in my heart. Amen.

DAY 317: TRUSTING IN GOD ALONE

Scripture:
"Blessed is the man who trusts in the Lord, whose trust is the Lord."

Jeremiah 17:7 ESV

Explanation:
You are blessed when you trust the Lord and let Him help you make every decision. When you give every decision to Him, you know He will guide you down the right path. He will give you the strength to go on when you feel you can't take another step. Trusting in God is much better than trusting in men because God will never lead you astray or let you down. He will always help you. Trusting in God will get you way farther than trusting in men.

Bedtime Prayer:
Dear God, help me always trust in you. Amen

DAY 318: SUCCESS IN JESUS

Scripture:
"Save us, we pray, O Lord! O Lord, we pray, give us success!"

Psalm 118:25 ESV

Explanation:
When was the last time you prayed, "Lord, please help me. Please give me success"? There is nothing wrong with asking God to help you accomplish your dreams, desires, and goals. There is nothing to be ashamed of in admitting that you need God's help. Cry out to Him from the depths of your heart and ask Him for wisdom, understanding, and knowledge as you take the following steps: changing schools from middle school to junior high, preparing for a big test, or trying out for varsity cheerleading captain.

Bedtime Prayer:
Dear God, please give me success in your name alone. Amen.

DAY 319: GOD IS YOUR SHEILD

Scripture:
"He stores up sound wisdom for the upright; he is a shield to those who walk in integrity."

Proverbs 2:7 ESV

Explanation:
God is your shield and place of refuge from all oppression and all harm. Whether you're experiencing bullying, losing friends, or people mocking you for your strong faith in Jesus, He is your shield and rampart. He is willing to shield you and not let people's mean and angry words take root in your mind, body, heart, or soul. No matter what, stand firm in your faith and walk with your head held high. Walk with integrity because Jesus is by your side.

Bedtime Prayer:

Dear God, thank you for being my everlasting shield. Amen.

DAY 320: FULFIL YOUR PLANS

Scripture:
"May he grant you your heart's desire and fulfill all your plans!"

Psalm 20:4 ESV

Explanation:
Are you trying to fulfill your plans on your own? How far did that get you? It is more important to make sure your plans align with God's plans. God will grant your heart's desires and fulfill His plan for your life in His timing and ways. When He shows you what He wants you to do with your life, follow His lead and see where He takes you. Ask Him to give you the knowledge as to what steps to take in every part of your life.

Bedtime Prayer:

Dear God, fulfill your plans for my life, not mine. Amen.

DAY 321: CALL OUT TO GOD

Scripture:
"Call to me and I will answer you, and will tell you great and hidden things that you have not known."

Jeremiah 33:3 ESV

Explanation:
If you've ever been afraid to cry out to God, you don't need to be fearful of Him. When you call to Him, He will answer you in His timing. When you ask Him for the knowledge to get through different phases of your life, He will tell you some great and hidden things you've never known before. Be careful what you do with that knowledge, though. Make sure you always use God's answers and His knowledge to help others realize the importance of having a relationship with God.

Bedtime Prayer:
Dear God, help me boldly call out to you. Amen.

DAY 322: WORSHIP IN SPIRIT AND TRUTH

Scripture:
"God is spirit, and those who worship him must worship in spirit and truth."

John 4:24 ESV

Explanation:
How do I worship God in spirit and truth? You might ask. It's simple. Just ask God to help you know how to worship Him with all your heart, soul, and mind. Go deep into your subconscious and forget everything except worshipping God fully in spirit and truth. Ask Him what the truth is in His eyes, and then go about your life speaking the truth at school, at church, at home, and around your community. See where He leads you to go and what He leads you to say.

Bedtime Prayer:
Dear God, please help me worship you in spirit and truth. Amen.

DAY 323: NEVER CHANGES HIS MIND

Scripture:
"God is not man, that he should lie, or a son of man, that he should change his mind."

Numbers 23:19 ESV

Explanation:
No matter what you've done, God never looks at you and says to Himself, "Oh no. Here she goes again! Will she ever learn?" No. He knew you would sin daily. When He said He would deliver you from sin and death, you can believe Him. Believe in His promises because He never changes His mind. He never lets anyone down, and He never will. He never lies either, so you can always trust Him and realize He knows you better than you know yourself.

Bedtime Prayer:
Dear God, thank you for never changing your mind about me. Amen.

DAY 324: THE ONLY GOD

Scripture:
"To the King of the ages, immortal, invisible, the only God, be honor and glory forever and ever. Amen."

1 Timothy 1:17 ESV

Explanation:
God is immortal, invisible. That means that no one can ever kill Him or cause Him to die. He will forever reign over the heavens and the earth. He is the only God that you should ever worship. Unfortunately, there are false gods in this world, but they are not even close to being more important than the one true God. You can do your part to show everyone that Jesus and God are the reason you are who you are. Worship Him and proclaim His goodness, honor, and glory.

Bedtime Prayer:
Dear God, I praise you because you're the only God. Amen.

DAY 325: RADIANCE OF GOD

Scripture:
"He is the radiance of the glory of God..."

Hebrews 1:3 ESV

Explanation:
Have you ever experienced the radiance of Jesus and God in all His glory? Maybe you've been at church, and the whole church was filled with light as soon as the worship music started. God shines His light on your life and the entire congregation. Maybe you've even sung in the children's choir and felt God's power come over you as you sang. You lifted your hands high. That's the power of the Holy Spirit at work within you. Jesus is the radiance and ultimate glory of God.

Bedtime Prayer:
Dear God, thank you that Jesus radiates your glory. Amen.

DAY 326: MERCIFUL GOD

Scripture:
"For the Lord your God is a merciful God. He will not leave you or destroy you..."

Deuteronomy 4:31 ESV

Explanation:
When was the last time you experienced God's mercy? Maybe you've felt His arms wrap you in a warm hug when things were tough for your family. You experience His mercy every day, believe it or not. That breath you just took, that's His mercy and grace. He gave you another day of life because He has a beautiful purpose for you. With everything you learn in school, He's helping you become more intelligent by the day. You can teach your family more about Him whenever you read His word.

Bedtime Prayer:
Dear God, thank you for not leaving or destroying me. Amen.

DAY 327: WALKING UPRIGHTLY

Scripture:
"No good thing does he withhold from those who walk up-rightly."

Psalm 116:5 ESV

Explanation:
Do you walk with integrity every day? That doesn't mean walking with your nose in the air like you have everything figured out. It just means to walk humbly before God, acknowledging that He is the only reason you have everything you have. Because you believe in God, He never leaves you hanging when you ask Him questions. He may not answer how you'd want or expect Him to, but He will not withhold anything from you. He doesn't withhold anything good from you.

Bedtime Prayer:

Dear God, help me to walk uprightly and honor you. Amen.

DAY 328: GOD'S WAYS ARE JUST

Scripture:
"The Rock, his work is perfect, for all his ways are justice."

Deuteronomy 32:4 ESV

Explanation:
God is the Rock of all ages. His work is entirely perfect. There's nothing He won't do for you as His child. His ways and His will are perfect. His justice is the best form because He will always prevail. He will give you justice if you're being bullied, such as online bullying, bullying for the way you talk, dress, act, or for the way you profess your faith in Jesus. He stands up for you and has your back in any form of bullying that you're dealing with.

Bedtime Prayer:

Dear God, thank you that I don't have to be perfect. Bring justice to earth. Amen

DAY 329: THE ONLY TRUE GOD

Scripture:
"And this is eternal life, that they know you, the only true God, and Jesus Christ whom you have sent."

John 17:3 ESV

Explanation:
How amazing is knowing that you have an eternal place in heaven waiting for you when your assignment on earth is complete? What an honor that Jesus came down from heaven to save you from your sins. To know there will be no more pain, sadness, or persecution in eternity. There will be God's perfect glory, and you will get to worship Him with your family. While on your assignment, worship Him as the one true God with everything you have.

Bedtime Prayer:

Dear God, teach me to help others know you as the one true God. Amen.

DAY 330: IMPOSSIBLE WITH MAN

Scripture:
"But he said, "What is impossible with man is possible with God."

Luke 18:27 ESV

Explanation:
You've probably had moments when you thought, "This is impossible. How am I ever going to get through this? God, where are you now?" Every kid and adult has said those things at one point or another. But the good news is that those thoughts are lying to you. Jesus said, "What is impossible with man is possible with God." Imagine Him in front of you saying, "Ha, my dear child, this might be impossible for you, but nothing has ever been impossible with me. Nor will anything ever be impossible."

Bedtime Prayer:

Dear God, thank you. What's impossible with me is possible for you. Amen.

DAY 331: GOD'S FREE GIFT

Scripture:
"For the wages of sin is death, but the free gift of God is eternal life in Christ Jesus our Lord."

Romans 6:23 ESV

Explanation:
Free gifts sound pretty amazing, right? Unfortunately, not everything that people promise you is free. The only gift that is totally free is from God. That's the gift of faith, salvation, and spending eternity in heaven with Jesus as your Lord and Savior. You were originally supposed to die for your sin, but Jesus loved you so much that He took all your guilt, sin, and shame upon Himself and forgave you. He gave you the free gift of life with Him forever.

Bedtime Prayer:

Dear God, thank you for giving me eternal life as a free gift. Amen.

DAY 332: BUILDER OF EVERYTHING

Scripture:
"(For every house is built by someone, but the builder of all things is God.)"

Hebrews 3:4 ESV

Explanation:
God is the builder of everything. He built the heavens, earth, moon, galaxies, and stars. Plus, all creatures and all humans on earth. Just like how your parents had someone build the house, God was also instrumental in building your parent's house because He gave the builders and construction workers the time, creativity, and ability to overcome many obstacles to make the home. God is the builder of everything in your life, from you to your family, friends, home, and pets. Everything is built by Him alone.

Bedtime Prayer:
Dear God, help remind me that you've built everything, including me. Amen.

DAY 333: JESUS, FULL OF GRACE

Scripture:

"We have seen his glory, glory as of the only Son from the Father, full of grace and truth. "

John 1:14 ESV

Explanation:

Jesus is the only one who is truly filled with unending grace and truth. You've seen His glory in the color of a sunrise or sunset, the stillness of the crisp fall air, seeing the ocean, or every time you hug the ones you love. Jesus extends His never-ending grace to you every day. He forgives you for your sins and helps you forgive those who've hurt you. He loves it when you talk to Him and get to know Him better. There is no one more gracious than Him.

Bedtime Prayer:

Dear God, please help me to know your grace and truth daily. Amen.

DAY 334: INVISIBLE ATTRIBUTES

Scripture:

"For his invisible attributes, namely, his eternal power and divine nature, have been clearly perceived."

Romans 1:20 ESV

Explanation:

God's invisible attributes are His eternal power, which means He will last forever. His divine nature is another invisible attribute. He can turn every lousy situation around in the blink of an eye, but He sometimes won't just to see how much you rely on Him. His invisible attributes have been named so you can begin to understand them better day by day. Ask Him to reveal His divine nature and eternal power in the way you need to know them.

Bedtime Prayer:

Dear God, help me to know your eternal power and divine nature. Amen.

DAY 335: GOD IS LIVING AND ACTIVE

Scripture:
"For the word of God is living and active, sharper than any two-edged sword..."

Hebrews 4:12 ESV

Explanation:
His word has been alive since the beginning of time and has changed many people's lives. It will continue to be the most important book anyone, including you, will ever read. Ask God to help you understand His word better with each passing day. Enjoy reading His word alone or in a group with your friends inside and outside school. It is sharper than any sword because it contains the truth you must know. God is blunt in His love and His discipline toward you.

Bedtime Prayer:

Dear God, please help me know that your word is alive and active in my life. Amen.

DAY 336: SHARPER THAN ANY SWORD

Scripture:
".... piercing to the division of soul and of spirit..."

Hebrews 4:12 ESV

Explanation:
God's word can pierce your soul and mind anytime. All you have to do is ask Him to reveal different things you haven't known. The things you learn from God will surprise you. He will help you see the difference between right and wrong by piercing the divisions in your body, such as the division of your soul and spirit. Your soul may not know that you're not supposed to do something sinful or dangerous. But your spirit will know and nudge you in the right direction.

Bedtime Prayer:

Dear God, teach me that your word is sharper than anyone's. It pierces the soul. Amen.

DAY 337: DISCERNING THOUGHTS AND INTENTIONS OF THE HEART

Scripture:

"discerning the thoughts and intentions of the heart."

Hebrews 4:12 ESV

Explanation:

When you don't know what you should do in a particular situation at home, at school, or during a sports practice, turn to God, saying, "Lord, help me understand what you want me to do. He already knows your heart's intentions and the thoughts in your mind. He knew them before you even existed and knows you better than anyone. So it's ok to cry out to Him, asking Him to reveal your heart's thoughts and intentions so you know what to do, think, and speak.

Bedtime Prayer:

Dear God, help me discern the intentions in people's hearts. Amen.

DAY 338: DIFFERENT NAMES OF GOD (PART 1)

Scripture:

"his name shall be called Wonderful Counselor, Mighty God, Everlasting Father, Prince of Peace."

Isaiah 9:6 ESV

Explanation:

God has many names. He is a wonderful counselor because He is ready, willing, and able to be there for you regardless of circumstances. He will counsel you at a moment's notice. He is the mighty God because His power is unfathomable. He is called the everlasting Father because He is your everlasting heavenly Father who knew you before you even existed. He is called the Prince of Peace because you will feel unimaginable, overwhelmingly wonderful peace when you feel His presence. He wants to surround you with His peace.

Bedtime Prayer:

Dear God, help me to know many of your wonderful names. Amen

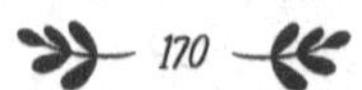

DAY 339: DIFFERENT NAMES FOR GOD (PART 2)

Scripture:
"I am the Alpha and the Omega," says the Lord God,"

Revelation 1:8 ESV

Explanation:
God is the Alpha and the Omega, which means He is the beginning and the end of everything. He existed before time began, made everything, and saw that it was beautiful. These names of Alpha and Omega are used for both God and Jesus because He sent Jesus as His one and only Son to save you from your sins and give you the chance to live with Him in eternity when you get called home to eternity. Worship Him as the Alpha and Omega every chance you get.

Bedtime Prayer:

Dear God, teach me that you have many names, including alpha and omega. Amen.

DAY 340: A THOUSAND GENERATIONS

Scripture:
"...God who keeps steadfast love with those who keep his commandments, to a thousand generations,"

Deuteronomy 7:9 ESV

Explanation:
When you follow God and keep His commandments, He will stay close to you. The commandments include keeping His name sacred and never worshiping any god except Him, keeping Sunday as the Sabbath day, honoring your father and mother, never killing, slandering, or hurting someone with your words, never cheating on your future spouse, and staying faithful, never stealing, never saying something false about your neighbor, and lastly never wanting what someone else has. He keeps His steadfast love close to your heart.

Bedtime Prayer:

Dear God, please keep your commands even unto a thousand generations. Amen.

DAY 341: HOW YOU SHOULD PRAY

Scripture:
"Pray then like this: "Our Father in heaven, hallowed be your name."

Mathew 6:9 ESV

Explanation:
This prayer is called "The Lord's Prayer." Suppose you've ever been nervous about coming before God. Pray like this: "Our Father who art in heaven. Hallowed be thy name. Thy kingdom come. Thy will be done, on earth as it is in heaven. Give us this day our daily bread and forgive us our trespasses as we forgive those who trespass against us. Lead us not into temptation, but deliver us from evil, for thine is the kingdom, the power, and the glory forever and ever. Amen.

Bedtime Prayer:

Dear God, help me pray as you taught me. Amen.

DAY 342: STRONG TOWER

Scripture:
"The name of the Lord is a strong tower; the righteous man runs into it and is safe."

Proverbs 18:10 ESV

Explanation:
You can always run to God and be safe in His arms anytime. His name is a strong tower you can always turn to, no matter what you go through. You will sin daily, but it doesn't mean you can't ever come to Him, no matter your feelings. Who wouldn't want a strong tower to run to when times get tough? You can go to Him at any time, day or night. You are always safe in His loving arms. His strength will never be broken.

Bedtime Prayer:

Dear God, thank you for being my strong tower forever. Amen.

DAY 343: SING PRAISES

Scripture:
"So will I ever sing praises to your name,"

Psalm 61:8 ESV

Explanation:
Even if you can't sing in key, you can still praise Him by singing to Him in church, at school, at recess, and on the sports team. You can enjoy it no matter where you are, what you do, or who you worship. Even if you don't have a good voice, God still loves to hear you lift your voice in prayer or praise, day or night. Every chance you get, praise Him and sing praises to His name.

Bedtime Prayer:

Dear God, help me to sing your praises forever. Amen.

DAY 344: GOD'S LOVE IS BETTER THAN LIFE

Scripture:
"Because your steadfast love is better than life, my lips will praise you."

Psalm 63:3 ESV

Explanation:
God's love is better than life itself because no one can ever love you in the same way God can. God deserves all the praise in the world for loving you and everyone else the way He does. We don't drive His love, but He gives it to you and everyone else freely. Every day, find something to praise God for, no matter how you feel or what you're going through. He loves you more than life because His love is greater than life itself.

Bedtime Prayer:

Dear God, thank you for your love, which is better than my life. Amen.

DAY 345: GOD WILL PROVIDE

Scripture:

"So Abraham called the name of that place, "The Lord will provide."

Genesis 22:14 ESV

Explanation:

In this Bible story, Abraham walked up the mountain to sacrifice his son Isaac because God had told him to do it. But right as he was about to kill his only son with a knife, God provided a ram for Abraham to sacrifice instead of his only son, Isaac. So Abraham built an altar in God's honor and praise. He called the name of the place, "The Lord will provide." Who wouldn't believe in a God like that? He saved Isaac from being sacrificed because of Abraham's faith.

Bedtime Prayer:

Dear God, please help me believe you'll provide for me. Amen.

DAY 346: DON'T USE GOD'S NAME IN VAIN

Scripture:

"You shall not swear by my name falsely, and so profane the name of your God: I am the Lord."

Leviticus 19:12 ESV

Explanation:

You shouldn't swear by using God's name in vain at any time. You shouldn't swear by His name falsely in any situation. But you're going to sin because you aren't perfect. No one is. Just ask Him to help you not to swear to or by God. Saying "oh my God" is using the name of the Lord's name in vain. But all you have to do is ask God to help you honor His name daily.

Bedtime Prayer:

Dear God, help me not to use your name in vain. Amen.

DAY 347: TAKE REFUGE IN GOD

Scripture:
"This God—his way is perfect...he is a shield for all those who take refuge in him."

Psalm 18:30 ESV

Explanation:
Isn't it amazing to know that you can take refuge in God when you're arguing with your friends or parents? You can come to Him any time and ask Him for the courage to try out for your school's sports team or for Him to give you the courage to try out for cheerleading. When you're struggling with school and don't know how to pass a test, ask Him to help you understand each subject better before each test.

Bedtime Prayer:
Dear God, help me always to take refuge in you. Amen.

DAY 348: GOD IS YOUR ROCK

Scripture:
"For who is God, but the Lord? And who is a rock except our God?"

2 Samuel 22:32 ESV

Explanation:
Isn't it amazing to know that God is and can be your rock in any situation? The rock is often where people build their foundation in life. Since you know God, God is your ultimate rock. God is your everlasting rock. You can always count on Him for everything. You can count on Him because He never fails, and He never crumbles or cracks under pressure the way we do. Build your life upon the rock that is higher than you.

Bedtime Prayer:
Dear God, thank you for being my rock and fortress. Amen.

DAY 349: GOD'S COUNSEL

Scripture:
"The counsel of the Lord stands forever..."

Psalm 33:11 ESV

Explanation:
Isn't it comforting that God is the ultimate wonderful counselor? You can always come to Him for guidance as you go through difficult times and different stages of your life. His mighty counsel stands forever. You'll never be led astray when talking to God. Ask Him which path you should take with school, participating in sports, and where you should volunteer at church. Let Him be your ultimate guide. Let His holy counsel be the only type you listen to when facing peer pressure.

Bedtime Prayer:

Dear God, thank you that I can turn to you for your everlasting counsel. Amen.

DAY 350: YOUR INHERITANCE

Scripture:
"In him we have obtained an inheritance..."

Ephesians 1:11 ESV

Explanation:
Do you know you have an inheritance from your parents and God? He automatically gave you your holy inheritance when you accepted Jesus as your Lord and Savior. That inheritance includes the greatest gifts you can ever receive. Nothing will ever come close to your salvation, faith, and eternity with Jesus in heaven forever! All because of Jesus' love for you, you are covered and saved by His precious blood and what He did for you on the cross.

Bedtime Prayer:

Dear God, thank you for giving me an inheritance through my faith in you. Amen.

DAY 351: BE WISE WITH YOUR WORDS

Scripture:
"There is one whose rash words are like sword thrusts..."

Proverbs 12:18 ESV

Explanation:
When the Bible says that rash words are like sword thrusts, God wants you to understand that words can go in and pierce your body, mind, and soul. Every time you say something rashly, you should think twice about how you say things. Do your best not to react rashly to anything your teachers, parents, coaches, or siblings say. Don't thrust your words onto someone's heart and leave them with gaping emotional wounds. Once you say stuff, it can't be taken back; it can only be forgiven.

Bedtime Prayer:

Dear God, please help me be wise and never rashly with my words. Amen

DAY 352: DELIGHT OF YOUR HEART

Scripture:
"your words became to me a joy and the delight of my heart..."

Jeremiah 15:16 ESV

Explanation:
Let God's word and promises become the joy and delight in your heart. You learn more about Him and yourself whenever you recite a new and exciting verse to your friends, family, coaches or teachers, and even your classmates. Let your words reflect God's love, grace, and mercy.

Bedtime Prayer:

Dear God, please help your words become my heart's delight. Amen.

DAY 353: DAY OF JUDGEMENT

Scripture:
"on the day of judgment, people will give account for every careless word they speak."

Mathew 12:36 ESV

Explanation:
It is terrifying to realize that everyone will give an account for the careless words they speak when they are all in front of God on judgment day. It should scare you into ensuring that you only talk nicely to your parents, don't gossip with friends in school, or bully others because of how they look, talk, or act. You will be accountable for everything you say on earth, so do your best to speak kindly, out of love, and encourage people instead of discouraging them.

Bedtime Prayer:
Dear God, please help me not to be careless with my words. Amen.

DAY 354: GUARD MY LIPS

Scripture:
"Set a guard, O Lord, over my mouth; keep watch over the door of my lips!"

Psalm 141:3 ESV

Explanation:
This verse is a prayer to God asking Him to guard your lips so you don't say anything hurtful, mean, regretful, or something that harms someone's reputation. It's asking God to guard your lips, and that's often a great thing to do. It's only admitting to God that, at times, your mouth just gets filled with fearful and outrageous thoughts, and you ask God for help in getting rid of them. There's nothing wrong with asking Him to guard your thoughts.

Bedtime Prayer:
Dear God, please guard my lips and heart. Amen.

DAY 355: SPEAK GENTLY

Scripture:
"A gentle tongue is a tree of life,"

Proverbs 15:4 ESV

Explanation:
It can be hard to be gentle with your words when you feel angry, sad, or uncertain. But the Bible says a gentle tongue is a tree of life. Instead of yelling at your siblings for entering your room without asking permission, invite them into your room anyway. If you're angry at your parents' rules about being home by 8 p.m. when playing with your friends, instead of shouting that their rules aren't fair, obey them. When you control your tongue and answer people gently, you're honoring God.

Bedtime Prayer:

Dear God, help me to speak wisely and gently no matter who I talk to. Amen.

DAY 356: ACCEPTABLE IN HIS SIGHT

Scripture:
"Let the words of my mouth and the meditation of my heart be acceptable in your sight..."

Psalm 19:14 ESV

Explanation:
This Bible verse is what you may hear in church when a pastor is about to start his sermon. But this verse can also be applied to your life. Throughout your day, ask God to help you know when to speak and when not to speak. Ask Him to help you understand how to approach people with kindness and love. Ask Him to help you have the words and thoughts be acceptable in His sight. God will help you know what to say and do to honor Him.

Bedtime Prayer:

Dear God, make my words and thoughts acceptable to you. Amen.

DAY 357: JUSTIFIED BY YOUR WORDS

Scripture:
"For by your words you will be justified,"

Mathew 12:37 ESV

Explanation:
You will be justified by your words, thoughts, deeds, and actions when you get to heaven. But you will be justified by your words on earth as well. God knows when and how you will sin before you ever do. But the word justified can mean "just as if you never sinned." You're justified and saved through faith because of God's love, mercy, and grace. Just ask God for forgiveness whenever you sin. Ask Him to help your words justify you.

Bedtime Prayer:
Dear God, Help me to be justified by my words, not condemned. Amen.

DAY 358: CONDEMNED BY WORDS

Scripture:
"by your words, you will be condemned."

Mathew 12:37 ESV

Explanation:
You have a choice of either being justified or condemned by your words if you don't ask God for forgiveness for the mean or out-of-character things you say to your parents, siblings, teachers, friends, or coaches. Just because you feel you're being wronged doesn't give you the right to be nasty to anyone. Remember, you can choose whether you're condemned or justified by your words. Wouldn't you instead honor God and others with your words rather than be condemned by Him for your words?

Bedtime Prayer:
Dear God, please help me not to be condemned by my words. Amen.

DAY 359: ALREADY MADE CLEAN

Scripture:
*"Already you are clean because of the word that I have spo-
ken to you."*

John 15:3 ESV

Explanation:
As soon as you ask God for forgiveness, no matter what
you've done, as long as you confess that you know you're
a sinner and need His help to repent, you're already made
clean by the blood of Jesus Christ when you ask for forgiveness. It's all because of the words Jesus spoke over your life.
He made you clean by His blood on the cross. You don't have
to worry about making yourself clean or about your past
mistakes.

Bedtime Prayer:

*Dear God, please speak your words and help make me clean.
Amen.*

DAY 360: THOSE WHO ARE PERISHING

Scripture:
*"For the word of the cross is folly to those who are perish-
ing..."*

1 Corinthians 1:18 ESV

Explanation:
Sadly, not everyone will accept Jesus as their Lord and Savior. Some people won't believe in Him no matter how hard
you try to help them believe in His goodness. Some people
will never believe that Jesus is real or that He died on the
cross for their sins. The words of the cross are folly to those
who are perishing. Just be Jesus' example and spread His
message in every way possible.

Bedtime Prayer:

*Dear God, help me to speak your words to those who don't
believe. Amen.*

DAY 361: SAVED BY GOD'S POWER

Scripture:

"...but to us who are being saved it is the power of God."

1 Corinthians 1:18 ESV

Explanation:

When you're interested in learning about God, you will want to learn more about Him by reading His word daily and asking your trusted friends, family members, and pastor about Him. You're saved by His power. Not just by His power, but by the power of His death on the cross and by the power of His words, "it is finished" on the cross. By saying, "It is finished," He took away every sin you've ever committed and put it upon Himself. That's the power of the cross.

Bedtime Prayer:

Dear God, please help me understand the power of the cross better. Amen.

DAY 362: TOO MANY WORDS

Scripture:

"When words are many, transgression is not lacking, but whoever restrains his lips is prudent."

Proverbs 10:19 ESV

Explanation:

Have you ever noticed that when you talk too fast or too much, you can't always watch your words or think fast enough about what you say? You can end up hurting yourself and others with your words unintentionally when you talk too much. This verse says that there are transgressions when there are too many words. The word transgressions means sins or mistakes. But when you keep your mouth shut, you're honoring God and keeping yourself out of needless drama.

Bedtime Prayer:

Dear God, please help me not to speak too many words. Amen.

DAY 363: YOUR WORD IN MY HEART

Scripture:
"I have stored up your word in my heart, that I might not sin against you."

Psalm 119:11 ESV

Explanation:
How do you store God's word in your heart? Take it a bit at a time: one subject, devotion, or verse. Find time to read the Bible before, during, or after school. Memorize your favorite poem. Then, post it in your planner, computer, or bedroom door, and recite it yourself. Store His word in your heart, and do your best not to sin against Him.

Bedtime Prayer:

Dear God, please help me always keep your word in my heart. Amen.

DAY 364: JESUS' WORDS

Scripture:
"Heaven and earth will pass away, but my words will not pass away."

Mathew 24:35 ESV

Explanation:
This Bible verse means that Jesus' beautiful words will never run out or cease to exist because Jesus is the Son of God, and His words are everlasting. Heaven and earth will pass away, but Jesus' words will last forever. Ask God to help you learn His words more and more daily. The more you know about Him, the more you will want to keep learning and share the things you learn about Jesus with others. Teach your younger siblings about the impact of Jesus' words.

Bedtime Prayer:

Dear God, please help me never to forget your words. Amen.

DAY 365: BOASTING ISN'T WORTH IT

Scripture:

"So also the tongue is a small member, yet it boasts of great things."

James 3:5 ESV

Explanation:

You probably have bragged or boasted in your life at one time or another. And you will most likely brag about other things in your life as you get older. The tongue is the smallest member of your body but has the power of life and death. Consider how bragging could make your friends, classmates, and even your extended family members feel. The only thing you should ever be boasting about is Jesus' love for you and others.

Bedtime Prayer:

Dear God, please help me not to boast about anything. Amen.

CONCLUSION

We hope this book brought both you and many other teens closer to God every week through the devotionals. We also hope the topics were easy to understand and come to terms with.

We praise God for making each young girl in His miraculous, beautiful image. Remember, there is nothing impossible with God. God has an excellent plan for each person's life.

We hope this book has inspired you and many others in different ways, such as teaching them how to pray, praise, and thank God for everything He has done in their lives.

Most of all, we pray that this book has helped you and other girls to forgive yourself and other people because God has forgiven you for all of your sins.